T0318316

Shakespeare
in Jest

Shakespeare in Jest draws fascinating parallels between Shakespeare's humour and contemporary humour. Indira Ghose argues that while many of Shakespeare's jokes no longer work for us, his humour was crucial in shaping comedy in today's entertainment industry.

The book looks at a wide variety of plays and reads them in conjunction with examples from contemporary culture, from stand-up comedy to late-night shows. Ghose shows the importance of jokes, the functions of which are often remarkably similar in Shakespeare's time and ours. Shakespeare's wittiest characters are mostly women, who use wit to puncture male pretensions and to acquire cultural capital. Clowns and wise fools use humour to mock their betters, while black humour trains the spotlight on the audience, exposing our collusion in the world it skewers. In a discussion of the ethics of humour, the book uncovers striking affinities between Puritan attacks on the theatre and contemporary attacks on comedy.

An enjoyable and accessible read, this lively book will enlighten and entertain students, researchers, and general readers interested in Shakespeare, humour, and popular culture.

Indira Ghose is Professor of English at the University of Fribourg, Switzerland. She has published widely on early modern wit, jesting, and laughter.

Spotlight on Shakespeare

Series Editors: John Garrison and Kyle Pivetti

Spotlight on Shakespeare offers a series of concise, lucid books that explore the vital purchase of the modern world on Shakespeare's work. Authors in the series embrace the notion that emergent theories, contemporary events, and movements can help us shed new light on Shakespeare's work and, in turn, his work can help us better make sense of the contemporary world. The aim of each volume is two-fold: to show how Shakespeare speaks to questions in our world and to illuminate his work by looking at it through new forms of human expression. *Spotlight on Shakespeare* will adopt fresh scholarly trends as contemporary issues emerge, and it will continually prompt its readers to ask, "What can Shakespeare help us see? What can he help us do?"

Spotlight on Shakespeare invites scholars to write non-exhaustive, pithy studies of very focused topics—with the goal of creating books that engage scholars, students, and general readers alike.

Available in this series:

Shakespeare in Jest
Indira Ghose

For more information about this series, please visit: www.routledge.com/Spotlight-on-Shakespeare/book-series/SOSHAX

INDIRA GHOSE

Shakespeare
in Jest

Routledge
Taylor & Francis Group

LONDON AND NEW YORK

First published 2022
by Routledge
2 Park Square, Milton Park, Abingdon, Oxon OX14 4RN

and by Routledge
605 Third Avenue, New York, NY 10158

Routledge is an imprint of the Taylor & Francis Group, an informa business

British Library Cataloguing-in-Publication Data
A catalogue record for this book is available from the British Library

Library of Congress Cataloging-in-Publication Data
A catalog record for this book has been requested

ISBN: 978-0-367-32246-5 (hbk)
ISBN: 978-0-367-32245-8 (pbk)
ISBN: 978-0-429-31750-7 (ebk)

DOI: 10.4324/9780429317507

Typeset in Joanna MT and Din
by Apex CoVantage, LLC

To Anthony Mortimer

Contents

List of figures   viii
Acknowledgements   x

Introduction   **1**

Joking relationships **One** **18**

Women and wit **Two** **49**

Clowns and wise fools **Three** **81**

Black humour **Four** **112**

Humour and ethics **Five** **143**

Further reading   174
Index   178

Figures

1.1 *Gran Torino* (2008), Dir. Clint Eastwood, produced
by Village Roadshow Pictures, Media Magik
Entertainment, and Malpaso Productions.   19

1.2 *Intolerable Cruelty* (2003), Dir. Ethan Coen, Joel
Coen, produced by Universal Pictures, Imagine
Entertainment (present), Alphaville Films (in
association with) (as Alphaville), Mike Zoss
Productions.   44

2.1 *Michelle Wolf: Joke Show* (2019), Dir. Lance Bangs,
produced by Irwin Entertainment.   54

2.2 *Aditi Mittal: Things They Wouldn't Let Me Say* (2017),
Dir. Fazilla Alana, produced by Netflix Studios.   69

3.1 *The Daily Show* (2019), Dir. Paul Pennolino,
produced by Comedy Central.   102

3.2 *The Death of Stalin* (2017), Dir. Armando Iannucci,
produced by Gaumont, Quad Productions,
Main Journey, France 3 Cinema, La Cie
Cinématographique, Panache Productions, AFPI,
Canal+, Ciné+, France Télévisions, Title Media.   106

4.1 *The Dark Knight* (2008), Dir. Christopher Nolan,
produced by Warner Bros. Pictures DC Comics,
Legendary Pictures, Syncopy.   118

4.2 *House of Cards, Chapter 14* (2014), Dir. Carl Franklin, produced by MRC, Trigger Street Productions, Wade/Thomas Productions, Knight Takes King Productions. 124

5.1 *Hannah Gadsby: Nanette* (2018), Dir. Madeleine Parry, Jon Olb, produced by Guesswork Television. 152

5.2 *Dave Chappelle: Sticks & Stones* (2019), Dir. Stan Lathan, produced by Pilot Boy Productions. 164

I am grateful to Antoinina Bevan-Zlatar, Emma Depledge, and Kilian Schindler for their thoughtful comments on various chapters. Walter Wuellenweber has been an indefatigable scout for contemporary comedy in all forms. Special thanks go to the students of my seminar on 'Renaissance Humour' and my lecture course on 'Why Shakespeare?' for their many invaluable tips.

In particular, I would like to thank my editors, John Garrison and Kyle Pivetti, for their suggestions, support, and encouragement. They are a dream team to work with.

My greatest debt is to Anthony Mortimer. This book is for him.

Introduction

In the Shakespeare spoof, *Upstart Crow*, Shakespeare, who harbours an inordinately high opinion of his genius, boasts to his wife about the funny scenes he has just written. His wife immediately deflates his enthusiasm. 'Will, I've told you, don't do comedy. It's not your strong point', she cautions him. Shakespeare remains adamant. He is particularly good at humour, he insists. 'It just requires lengthy explanation and copious footnotes. If you do your research, my stuff is actually really funny.'[1]

A running gag of the sitcom is how bad Shakespeare's jokes are. While he himself is convinced he will make comic history, all the other characters groan at his tedious witticisms and convoluted puns. When Kate, his landlord's daughter, is uncertain whether he means something seriously, and asks, 'Are you joking?' Bottom, his servant, butts in: 'Could well be. It's not funny. That's a good sign.'[2] The comedy mines Shakespeare's alleged lack of humour to hilarious effect. It riffs off topics like Shakespeare's often implausible plots (Shakespeare's friends burst out laughing when they hear what happens in *Hamlet*, congratulating him on his best comedy ever), and strews in fantasy words that sound vaguely Shakespearean ('puffling pants' or 'saucy prancings'). In addition, the show is saturated with in-jokes about the entertainment industry of today, as in the cameo appearance of a doleful-looking player

DOI: 10.4324/9780429317507-1

called 'Wolf Hall', who denies Shakespeare wrote his plays—an allusion to the star Shakespearean actor Mark Rylance, who plays Thomas Cromwell in the filmed version of Hilary Mantel's *Wolf Hall*. Rylance is actively involved in the Shakespeare authorship controversy and claims that the plays were written by the Earl of Oxford.

For all the fun it pokes at Shakespeare's terrible jokes, *Upstart Crow* mimics the comedic strategies that Shakespeare himself uses. Shakespeare often resorts to devices such as parody, verbal inventiveness, arch allusions to contemporary cultural developments, and self-reflexive jokes, playing games with the workings of humour. A case in point is the play-within-a-play in *A Midsummer Night's Dream*. It is a parodic version of the tragic classical myth of Pyramus and Thisbe, and brims with linguistic jokes, as in the outrageously garbled Prologue, or in its bombastic riot of alliteration ('He bravely broach'd his boiling breast', 5.1.146).[3] The play-within-a-play has fun lampooning other actors and their ineptitude, showing how they solemnly toil to capture real life (for instance, by consulting an almanac to know whether there will be a moon on the night of the performance), only to undermine any illusion of verisimilitude with their bumbling antics: an actor enters armed with props, who stolidly informs the audience, 'the lantern is the moon, I the man i'th' moon, this thornbush my thornbush, and this dog my dog' (247–49). By mocking the disastrous failure of the performance, the playlet reflects on how dramatic illusion works in practice—not by striving for realism at all costs, but by inviting the audience to undertake a foray into an imaginative sphere. At the same time, 'Pyramus and Thisbe' demonstrates how literalism offers ideal subject matter for humour.

This book argues that even if today we mightn't find many of Shakespeare's jokes funny, taking a closer look at his humour helps us understand how comedy works in contemporary life. It also reveals to what extent contemporary comic entertainment has been shaped by Shakespeare's variety of humour. Film directors, stand-up comics, and late-night show hosts have liberally helped themselves to comic ideas and motifs from his plays, adapting them for our times. These techniques are not necessarily Shakespeare's invention, but due to his iconic cultural status, they have been passed down through the ages and widely disseminated, providing templates for the comic artefacts of contemporary popular culture. Shakespeare had a decisive influence on the entertainment culture of his time—which for its part set the paradigm for today's entertainment industry. Shakespeare's humour helps us probe our own age: it sheds a light on the mechanisms of comedy today.

This book also looks at the culture of jesting in Shakespeare's world. In the sixteenth century, the term 'jest', which originally meant a tale of exploits, took on the meaning of a joke or prank. It additionally carried the connotations of play, a realm of the non-serious.[4] The joking situations in the plays mirror those of our society to a surprising extent. Shakespeare's plays are thronged with smart young men and women keen to show off their wit and cut each other down to size. Wit is deployed as a weapon in a relentless game of one-upmanship. Remarkably, in a society in which eloquence in women was frowned upon, most of Shakespeare's witty characters are women. Their legacy is reflected in a surge of vibrant female comedy in the contemporary world. The plays are also peopled by an array of professional entertainers, ranging from clowns to wise fools, whose modern counterparts are stand-up comedians and late-night hosts. Shakespeare's plays do not only feature the antics of bumbling but sly rustics, or the caustic wit of wise fools, but are frequently shot through with dark humour. The influence of Shakespeare's malevolent jesters can be traced in figures in popular culture such as the Joker in the *Dark Knight* series, President Underwood in *House of Cards*, the hitmen in *Fargo*, and the ineffectual suicide bombers in *Four Lions*. A final section of the book explores the implications of the term 'jest' in the context of a discussion of humour and ethics, and argues that there are affinities between the playful make-believe involved in jesting and the metadramatic reflections that thread Shakespeare's work. Jesting, I argue, involves the willingness to adopt an 'as if' frame in which nothing is quite what it seems, and different rules apply than in real life.

In analysing humour, our persistent focus on the content of jokes is, I believe, misguided. In comedy, context is key: who is making the joke, to whom, in which situation, determines whether a joke is funny or not. Jesting is a social activity. There is no essence of humour—it is the laughter in response to a jest that defines a situation or utterance as comic. It is true that jokes draw on comic conventions, stock motifs, and humorous cues, but what is crucial is the work that a joke does in a given situation. Investigating how contemporary humour operates also helps us understand Shakespeare's comedy. It gives us an insight into how Shakespeare uses humour to create a wide range of effects.

These effects are strikingly similar for both Shakespeare's time and ours. In Shakespeare's plays, jokes are used in the context of power relations, as implements of warfare to devastate others, or as a ploy in gamesmanship between rivals. Jokes are also utilised as a defence mechanism to defuse fear or anxiety. Alternatively, humour operates as a social lubricant and forges bonds between those involved in a jesting scenario, promoting cohesion within a community by endorsing shared values—a cohesion often built upon the exclusion of outsiders. Wit is employed to enhance the prestige of characters in the eyes of their peers, or as a seduction gambit, as a satirical tool, or as an instrument of power. By mocking deviations from social conventions, jokes disseminate advice concerning normative behaviour, and in this way reinforce communal values. Or jokes are simply a source of pleasure, for the characters in the play as well as for the audience. At times, Shakespeare proposes humour as a mode of survival, or a technique of resilience. Paradoxically, despite drawing our attention to the fact that we are a joke, Shakespeare's humour can also serve to affirm life as it is—and celebrate our imaginative powers. In the face of an absurd universe, the plays suggest, sometimes humour is all we have.

RENAISSANCE THEORIES OF HUMOUR

In Shakespeare's time, the dominant view was that humour was enmeshed with derision. This notion was rooted in classical theories of humour.[5] Aristotle's book on the genre of comedy is lost, but in the few remaining remarks in the *Poetics*, he defines the laughable as 'one category of the shameful' [sometimes translated as 'the ugly']. As he explains (rather cryptically), 'the laughable comprises any fault or mark of shame [sometimes translated as 'ugliness'] which involves no pain or destruction'.[6] Cicero reprises this idea and writes, 'The seat, the region, so to speak, of the humorous . . . lies in a certain dishonourableness and ugliness.'[7] Cicero spells out what Aristotle might mean, and what the limits of humour are. Heinous crimes are not funny, but shocking. The audience response should be indignation, not pleasure. Great suffering is not an appropriate topic for jokes either, but for sympathy. (He also has his speaker on wit, Gaius Julius

Caesar Strabo, point out that it would be imprudent to crack jokes about those who are very popular.) The best subject matter for jokes 'consists of defects found in the lives of people who are neither well esteemed nor wretched nor give the impression that some crime has earned them immediate punishment' (2.238). Cicero himself went on to break every rule Caesar has just expounded. For his fondness for jokes, he was sneered at by his enemies as 'the consular wag'.[8] Unfortunately for us, a collection of his jokes, compiled by his secretary, Tiro, is lost.

When the ancients speak of 'ugliness', it might be useful to remember that classical thought was grounded in the assumption of a universal order governed by the principles of reason, order, and harmony. What was deemed 'ugly' and earned ridicule was behaviour that transgressed the harmonious, rational order—that is, foolish and irrational behaviour. By acquiring knowledge and leading a virtuous life, ancient philosophers of virtually all stripes believed, humans could live in harmony with the rational order of the universe. These premises were radically rejected by the strand of Christianity that was most influential during the Reformation, the thought of the fourth-century Church Father, St Augustine, who had emphasised the fallen state of humankind and our dependence on divine grace, not our own actions, to achieve access to the truth. The deep flaw at the heart of classical ethics, Augustine believed, was to claim self-sufficiency in the human quest for virtue. The classical ideas about universal harmony would flourish anew during the eighteenth century, this time in a Christian guise, but during the early modern period, they were repudiated from an orthodox point of view—although, due to the prestige accorded to antiquity, they continued to circulate. What remained valid, however, for ancients as for early moderns, was the belief that ridicule was the high art of humour.

This was an art that needed to be carefully cultivated by dint of rhetorical training. Rhetorical manuals such as Thomas Wilson's *Art of Rhetoric* (1560) are quite clear about the skill involved in deflating others. Noting indignantly that 'some think it a trifle to have this gift, and so easy that every varlet or common jester is able to match with the best', Wilson points out that 'they which wittily can be pleasant [humorous], and when time serveth can give a merry answer or use a nipping taunt, shall be able to abash a right worthy man and make him at his wit's end through the sudden quip and unlooked frump given'.[9] Humour is war by other means, he avers. Shakespeare and his contemporaries had an astonishingly rich vocabulary for ridicule. George Puttenham's *Art of English Poesy* abounds in figures of speech like '*Ironia*, or the Dry Mock', '*Sarcasmus*, or the Bitter Taunt', '*Asteismus*, or the Merry Scoff', '*Micterismus*, or the Fleering Frump', '*Antiphrasis*, or the Broad Flout', and '*Charientismus*, or the Privy Nip'.[10] These are not Puttenham's invention, but lifted from his sources, in particular the comprehensive compendium of tropes first published in Latin by the humanist scholar, Joannes Susenbrotus, in 1540. It was probably used by Shakespeare at school.

Mockery was not, however, the only form of humour on offer in the Renaissance. Erasmus and his friend, Sir Thomas More, were among a group of thinkers who took a different attitude towards jesting, defending the practice as a source of recreation and a means to refresh the mind. They draw on Aristotle too, but this time on the *Nicomachean Ethics*. In the final book of the *Nicomachean Ethics*, Aristotle concedes that relaxation is an indispensable element in life, not as an end in itself, but to fortify us in the pursuit of virtue.[11] This idea also furnished thinkers such as Aquinas with a defence of humour, keen as he was to recuperate wit (or *eutrapelia*) from the strictures of St Paul, who had condemned jesting: 'Neither filthiness, nor foolish talking, nor jesting, which are not convenient: but rather giving of thanks' (Eph. 5:4, *KJV*). The Church Fathers frowned upon frivolity and indecorous levity, but Aquinas argues that moderate and decorous jesting is much to be recommended for its recreational value.[12]

For Aristotle, wittiness is one of the three social virtues, together with affability and truthfulness (by which he meant being truthful about one's own qualities, with a preference for understatement rather than boasting). It was Aristotle too who first explicitly introduced an element that has always shadowed the issue of humour: class. He labels those who carry jesting to excess 'vulgar buffoons', while those who can neither make nor take a joke are 'boorish and unpolished'. Tasteful humour, on the other hand, is the attribute of the 'refined and well-bred man'.[13]

There was also a venerable tradition commending laughter as conducive to good health, reaching back to Hippocrates. In his encyclopaedic *Anatomy of Melancholy* (1621), the scholar Robert Burton endorses mirth as a cure for melancholy. He recommends humorous discourse, jests, conceits, merry tales, as well as sports, plays, and merry company.[14] In the Prologue to his popular schoolboy play, *Roister Doister* (1566), Nicholas Udall promises to provide wholesome entertainment, and sets out the benefits of mirth: 'For Myrth prolongeth lyfe, and causeth health./Mirth recreates our spirites and voydeth pensivenesse.'[15] This is the root of the myth that laughter is the best medicine.

Udall also maintains that 'Mirth increaseth amitie', underlining the paradox that jesting can serve as a weapon to attack others as well as to facilitate amicable social relations. In the Preface to his *Apophthegms*, part of which were translated into English by Udall, Erasmus makes a similar point. Eramus' extensive collection of apophthegms, which became a Renaissance bestseller, consisted of witty anecdotes about famous figures from history, largely drawn from Plutarch's *Moralia*. Erasmus notes that mirth and relaxation are conducive 'for all maner compaignie kepyng among mene'.[16] He highlights the fact that humour is a social affair that, at its best, works to foster commonality.

EARLY MODERN JESTING

Both Erasmus and More were avid collectors of jokes. Erasmus himself wrote a small jestbook, the *Convivium fabulosum*, and More a comic poem, *A Merry Jest*. More acquired a reputation as a wag and became the subject of numerous witty anecdotes which entered jestbook lore after his death. A handful of these feature in the play *Sir Thomas More*, probably written in 1593 by Anthony Munday in collaboration with Henry Chettle, Thomas Dekker, and possibly Shakespeare. The play presents More jesting all the way to his death and includes the quip he made to the sheriff just before mounting the scaffold: 'I prithee, honest friend, lend my thy hand/To help me up. As for my coming down,/Let me alone, I'll look to that myself.'[17] More's brother-in-law, the printer and playwright John Rastell, produced the first English jestbook, *A Hundred Merry Tales* (1526). Rastell, along with the dramatist John Heywood, who also married into the More family, belongs to a set of intellectuals around More who took pleasure in collecting jokes, quips, and riddles, which they relished as a means to explore paradox, wordplay, the indeterminacy of language, and fallacious reasoning.[18] The first Renaissance jestbook, the *Facetiae*, published in 1470, is attributed to the Humanist scholar and papal secretary Poggio Bracciolini, and was a compendium of amusing tales that Poggio had swapped with colleagues and friends at the Vatican. Poggio dubbed the club of jest-lovers the 'bugiale', or 'factory of lies'.

The most popular butts of jestbook jokes are corrupt priests, lascivious women, and ignorant rustics. *A Hundred Merry Tales* contains the following joke:

> A preacher in the pulpit which preached the Word of God and, among other matters, spoke of men's souls, and said they were so marvellous and so subtle that a thousand souls might dance in the space of a nail of a man's finger. Among which audience, there was a merry conceited fellow of small devotion, that answered and said thus:
>
> 'Master doctor, if that a thousand souls may dance on a man's nail, I pray you tell then, where shall the piper stand?'
>
> *By this tale a man may see that it is but folly to show or to teach virtue to them that have no pleasure nor mind thereto.*[19]

The tongue-in-cheek tagline declares this to be a joke about the ignorance of the congregation, and Humanists would have enjoyed the literal-minded response of the jest-cracker. But it is just as likely to be a jibe at the metaphysical speculations of the scholastics, with a mocking glance at the abstruse (if apocryphal) line of inquiry, 'How many angels can dance on the head of a pin?'[20] Scholastics or the 'school men' were the *bêtes noires* of Humanists like Erasmus and Thomas More, who would have been delighted at a joke scoffing at the more arcane endeavours of the discipline of angelology. Jokes are notoriously slippery, however, and can be re-deployed by different social groups to suit their own purposes. Later in the century, the very same joke would be pressed into service by the strongly Protestant Thomas Wilson, who changes the preacher into a wandering friar to sharpen his barb at Catholicism.[21]

Jests were not only a matter of lampooning one's opponents, and a pleasant diversion for Humanists. They also served other functions. Take, for instance, the following joke, a favourite with early moderns:

> There came unto Rome a certaine young Gentleman very lyke unto Augustus, whome when the Emperour had seene, he demaunded of him if his mother had somtime beene at Rome or not? No quod the Gentleman, but my father hath beene often.[22]

It features in a book called *The Schoolemaster, or Teacher of Table Philosophie* (1576), and belongs to the popular group of jokes that centre on witty rulers, famous for their bon mots and clever ripostes as well as for being able to take a joke in good humour. In this case, the tables are deftly turned on Augustus by his anonymous but witty interlocutor, whose swift retort elegantly lobs the insinuation about his illegitimate birth back to the great man's side of the court. Jokes about famous people were much in demand, and the volume serves up a large number of anecdotes of this kind, assiduously set out in order of precedence: jests about emperors and kings before jests about earls, knights, squires, merchants, usurers, husbandmen, Jews, thieves, jesters, women, and fools, followed by jests about popes, cardinals, bishops, and monks.

The Schoolemaster is largely a translation of an earlier volume, the *Mensa philosophica*, which first appeared in print in 1470 and experienced a new spurt of popularity in the late fifteenth and early sixteenth century. But the joke itself is far older. It is recounted by the fifth-century imperial administrator, Macrobius, whose *Saturnalia* offers a rich trove of ancient Roman lore. Compiled against the backdrop of a Roman empire in its death throes and infused with nostalgia for the old order, the book celebrates three evenings of cultivated dinner conversation during the feast of Saturnalia. Each member of the party takes turns in telling a joke attributed to an ancient authority. One of them is the anecdote about Augustus and the witty retort by his look-alike.[23]

It is Macrobius' text that furnishes the template for the large number of the strange miscellanies, like *The Schoolemaster*, that early moderns were so fond of, in which jests jostle with riddles, puns, shaggy dog stories, and grave theological questions. The fact that the jokes were stale and endlessly recycled was irrelevant. Originality is not what the crackers of jokes were aiming for. On the contrary: citing earlier jokes added cachet to one's discourse. It was by contributing amusing stories about important people and displaying one's knack for the cut and thrust of repartee that one made one's mark in conversation and acquired a reputation for being quick-witted and entertaining. Humour became a form of cultural capital, an asset that allowed one to ascend the social scale. Or so many hoped. Social aspirants assiduously collected jokes and witticisms and honed their skills in badinage, in the hope of gaining prestige and securing access to the rich pickings associated with upward mobility.

The courtier Sir William Cornwallis was appalled at the attempts of social climbers to peddle humour. In his *Essayes*

(1600), he writes about upstarts 'that never utter any thing of their owne, but get Jestes by heart, and robbe bookes, and men of prettie tales, and yet hope for this to have a roome above the Salt'. It was customary to put a large salt cellar in the middle of a long table. Those given places at the top half of the dining board were considered guests of higher rank than those at the lower part of the table. Wit-crackers hoped to impress the company with their social skills and worm their way into the charmed circle of the elite. Cornwallis' irritation is palpable. 'I am tyred with these fellows', he writes.[24]

HUMOUR AND THE ENTERTAINMENT INDUSTRY

Shakespeare's age saw the birth of a culture industry for entertainment. Religious reformers launched a campaign to reform manners and combat all forms of idolatry. With the proscription of religious drama and festivity, a burgeoning market for entertainment and leisure emerged, which included the commercial theatre and cheap print. Humour was a staple of the entertainment industry, and it was retailed as a commodity in the theatre as well as the marketplace of print. Both jestbooks and plays were churned out by a rising professional class of hack writers and university wits, catering to a voracious appetite for comedy. An insatiable demand for humour is a feature our age shares with Shakespeare's, although our popular media are visual and digital: film, sit-coms, stand-up comedy, cartoons, and memes.

Jestbooks developed into a variety of self-help literature, providing their buyers with a storehouse of wit and amusing anecdotes to be sprinkled in conversation. Apart from jestbooks, jests are to be found in rhetorical manuals, conversational guides, miscellanies, and courtesy books.[25] There was plenty of vitriolic humour in circulation, particularly in religious polemic, but it played itself out in other genres. In jestbooks, controversial topics were largely avoided; the recreational value of the books was foregrounded. In their jestbook, *Jests to make you Merie* (1607), Thomas Dekker and George Wilkins begin with a description of the jest, stating, 'It is a weapon wherewith a foole does oftentimes fight, and a wise man defends himselfe by. It is the foode of good companie if it bee seasoned with judgment: but if with too much tartnesse, it is hardly digested but turns to quarrel.'[26] Their culinary image evokes a convivial setting; they advocate the use of humour as a means to promote camaraderie and good fellowship. In line with classical models, jests became shorter and the punchlines pithier. The jestbook was a distinctly urban genre, catering to an audience who appreciated the value of quick-witted ripostes and improvisation in London life— often the same gallants who flocked to the theatre.

Playwrights plundered material from jestbooks to lure gallants to the theatre. Thomas Dekker and John Webster, for instance, based the plot of *Northward Ho* on a story taken from *A Hundred Merry Tales*. At the same time, the plays made fun of the gallants thronging the theatres and jotting down jokes and witticisms in their commonplace books. In the Induction to *The Malcontent*, players parody members of the audience keen to show off their cultural savvy. A real actor, William Sly, a member of Shakespeare's theatre company, the King's Men, plays an affected gallant who tries to import the habits of private theatres into the Globe. He insists on having a seat on the stage, a practice that was accepted at private playhouses, but not in the public theatre, and demands to talk to the stars of the show: Harry Condell, Dick Burbage—and Will Sly. Boasting that he virtually knows the play by heart, he proudly holds up his notes: 'I have most of the jests here in my table-book.'[27]

In the First Quarto of *Hamlet*, the Prince too scoffs at the dim-witted spectators who indiscriminately jot down jests in their notebooks. Complaining about tedious jesters who repeat the same set of jokes, he notes, 'gentlemen quotes [*sic*] his jests down in their tables before they come to the play, as thus: "Cannot you stay till I eat my porridge?" and "You owe me a quarter's wages" and "My coate wants a cullison" and "Your beer is sour" and, blabbering with his lips and thus keeping in his cinquepace of jests, when, God knows, the warm clown cannot make a jest unless by chance, as the blind man catcheth a hare.'[28]

Hamlet, no mean jokesmith himself, is poking fun at the stale jests bandied about by stage clowns. Mocking the atrocious jokes of other comedians is something *Upstart Crow* picked up from Shakespeare, too. In this book, we will be tracing further patterns between Shakespeare's humour and contemporary humour, and looking at the dialogue sparked off between his work and today's comedy. What this book will not be doing, however, is analysing the jokes themselves with lengthy explanation and copious footnotes. Explaining a joke, as the writer E. B. White once said, is like dissecting a frog. You might understand it better, but in the process, the frog dies.[29]

NOTES

1 *Upstart Crow*, Season 1, Episode 1, written by Ben Elton, dir. Matt Lipsey and Richard Boden, perf. David Mitchell, Liza Tarbuck, Rob Rouse, Gemma Whelan (BBC Two, 2016–2018).

2 Ibid., Season 3, Episode 1.

3 References to the plays are taken from *The Norton Shakespeare*, ed. Stephen Greenblatt et al. (New York: W. W. Norton, 2016). All further references are in parentheses.

4 'jest, n.', *Oxford English Dictionary Online*.

5 The classic discussion is Quentin Skinner, 'Hobbes and the Classical Theory of Laughter', in *Visions of Politics*, Vol. 3 (Cambridge: Cambridge University Press, 2002), 142–76.

6 Aristotle, *Poetics*, trans. Stephen Halliwell, Loeb Classical Library (Cambridge, MA: Harvard University Press, 1995), 1449a33–5. Although the *Poetics* was only rediscovered in the late fifteenth century, earlier centuries had access to Aristotelian ideas through the commentaries by Averroes, translated into Latin in the thirteenth century.

7 Cicero, *On the Ideal Orator*, trans. James M. May and Jakob Wisse (New York: Oxford University Press, 2001), 2.236. All further references in parentheses.

8 Macrobius, *Saturnalia*, trans. Robert A. Kaster, Loeb Classical Library (Cambridge, MA: Harvard University Press, 2011), 2.1.12.

9 Thomas Wilson, *The Art of Rhetoric* (1560), ed. Peter E. Medine (University Park, PA: The Pennsylvania State University Press, 1994), 164.

10 *The Art of English Poesy* by George Puttenham: A Critical Edition, ed. Frank Whigham and Wayne A. Rebhorn (Ithaca: Cornell University Press, 2007), 273–76.

11 Aristotle, *The Nicomachean Ethics*, trans. David Ross, Oxford World's Classics (Oxford: Oxford University Press, 2009), 1176b.

12 St Thomas Aquinas, *Summa Theologiae*, Vol. 44, ed. and trans. Thomas Gilby (London: Blackfriars, 1972), 2a2ae, q. 168.

13 Aristotle, *The Nicomachean Ethics*, 1128a. The section on wittiness is 4.8.

14 Robert Burton, *The Anatomy of Melancholy*, ed. Thomas C. Faulkner, Nicolas K. Kiessling, and Rhonda L. Blair (Oxford: Clarendon, 1989), Part 2, Sect. 2, Memb. 6, Subsec. 4.

15 Nicholas Udall, [*Roister Doister*] *What creature is in health, eyther yong or olde* (1566), A2r. In quotations from early modern texts u/v and i/j have been modernised.

16 Desiderius Erasmus, *Apophthegmes*, trans. Nicholas Udall (1542), ***2v.

17 Anthony Munday and Others, *Sir Thomas More*, ed. Vittorio Gabrieli and Giorgio Melchiori, The Revel Plays (Manchester: Manchester University Press, 1990), 5.4.53-5.

18 Anne Lake Prescott, 'Humanism in the Tudor Jestbook', *Moreana* XXIV.95–96 (1987): 5–16.

19 John Rastell, *A Hundred Merry Tales: The Shakespeare Jest Book*, ed. John Thor Ewing (Edinburgh: Welkin Books, 2018), 254.

20 Peter Harrison, 'Angels on Pinhead and Needles' Points', *Notes and Queries* 63 (2016): 45–47. Harrison points out that the idea that medieval scholastics spent their time musing about angels dancing on pinheads is probably a seventeenth-century invention by the Protestant divine William Sclater.

21 Wilson, *The Art of Rhetoric*, 174.

22 *The Schoolemaster or Teacher of Table Philosophie* (1576), O4r.

23 Macrobius, *Saturnalia*, 2.4.20. Versions of the joke can be found in all ages. It was even recycled by Freud in his *Jokes and Their Relation to the Unconscious*, trans. James Strachey (New York: W. W. Norton, 1960), 79–80. See Barbara C. Bowen, ed., *One Hundred Renaissance Jokes: An Anthology* (Birmingham, AL: Summa Publications, 1988), 21.

24 Sir William Cornwallis, *Essayes* (1600), I3r.

25 The joke about Augustus, for instance, appears in Stefano Guazzo's *Civile Conversation* (1574). See *The Civile Conversation of M. Steeven Guazzo*, trans. George Pettie and Bartholomew Young (1581–86; London: Constable and Co., 1925), Bk. 1, 72.

26 Thomas Dekker and George Wilkins, *Jests to Make You Merie* (1607), B1r.

27 John Marston, *The Malcontent*, ed. George K. Hunter, Revels Student Editions (Manchester: Manchester University Press, 2000), Ind. 15–16. The play was written in 1602 for a boys' company, the Children of the Queen's Revels, and was staged at a private theatre, the Blackfriars Theatre. The Induction, probably written by John Webster, was added in 1603–4, when the play transferred to an adult company, the King's Men, based at the Globe. See Hunter, 'Introduction', 6–7.

28 *The Tragical History of Hamlet, Prince of Denmark*, First Quarto, Sc. 9, 28–35.

29 E. B. White, 'Preface', in *A Subtreasury of American Humor*, ed. E. B. White and Katharine S. White (New York: Coward-McCann, 1941), xvii.

One

'A set of wit well played'

Love's Labour's Lost 5.2.29

Two men walk into a salon. One is a young man, the other an old man. The old man tells the young man that he'll now learn how guys talk. He should listen carefully while he and his old friend Martin, the barber, banter with each other. What follows is a volley of insults:

Walt: How ya doing, Martin, you crazy Italian prick?

Martin: Walts! You cheap bastard! I should have known you'd come in, I was having such a pleasant day.

Walt: What'd you do? You ruse some poor blind guy out of his money? Gave him the wrong change?

Walt turns to the youth, Thao, and explains, 'You see kid, now that's how guys talk to one another.' He instructs him to re-enter the barber's shop and practise what he's just learned. When Thao does so and repeats the exact words that Walt used, the barber picks up a gun and threatens to blow his head off, while the appalled Walt remonstrates, 'You don't just come in and insult the man in his own shop!'

The humour of the scene lies in the fact that Thao gets it all wrong while getting it all right. In the film *Gran Torino*, the

DOI: 10.4324/9780429317507-2

fatherless youth Thao (played by Bee Vang) is befriended by the curmudgeonly Korean war veteran Walt (played by Clint Eastwood), who takes him under his wing (Figure 1.1).[1] In an attempt to instil self-confidence into the boy, Walt coaches him in how to behave in social situations. In this sequence, Walt teaches him that among old acquaintances, bandying jibes back and forth is a form of camaraderie, while the very same words used by a stranger are perceived as an act of hostility. Joking needs to be learned: in humour, context is key.

In the film narrative, Thao, a member of the society of Hmong immigrants who fled to the United States from Laos in the wake of the Vietnam War, is an outsider. He is bullied by the other youths who are members of the gang that terrorises his family and is initiated into adulthood by his old neighbour, Walt. In a different scenario, no doubt Thao would have learned the same lesson in his own community. 'Joking relationships', a term coined by the British anthropologist Alfred Radcliffe-Brown based on his field work in South African indigenous communities, are in fact widespread throughout the world.[2] He observed that potentially fraught relations, either between superior and

Figure 1.1 *Gran Torino* (2008), Dir. Clint Eastwood, produced by Village Roadshow Pictures, Media Magik Entertainment, and Malpaso Productions

inferior members of a group or between peers, are often negotiated in the form of formalised mockery of one party by the
other, or both simultaneously. Tensions are channelled into joking; affable relations are mediated in the form of taunts.

Bouts of ritualised abuse, known as 'flyting', are also a hallmark of festivity in Europe in the Middle Ages, and continued to
be a part of carnival celebrations in the early modern era.[3] With
the decline of carnival culture in Reformation England under
the pressure of a wide-reaching campaign to reform manners,
Shakespeare's age saw the birth of a commercial entertainment
industry, of which the theatre was a primary pillar. As numerous critics have noted, remnants of popular customs, including
flyting, have left their traces on early modern drama in a variety
of ways.[4] What is noteworthy, however, is the emergence of a
new element: the premium laid on verbal wit.

A play that, like Gran Torino, turns on the relationship between
a youth and his older mentor, and that contains elements of
a coming-of-age narrative, is Henry IV Part 1. Falstaff, probably
the wittiest figure in the gallery of Shakespearean characters,
is anything but a role model for a young prince, as Hal's father
and the Lord Chief Justice never tire of pointing out. A thief,
a braggart, and entirely free of moral scruples, he nonetheless
serves as a teacher to Hal, instructing him in the ways of the
world. One of the skills that Falstaff teaches Hal is how to jest.
The fat knight assumes the role of rhetorical sparring partner
for the future ruler, enabling him to hone his prowess in the
art of fast-paced quips and clever retorts. As Falstaff himself,
not overly prone to false modesty, notes, 'I am not only witty
in myself but the cause that wit is in other men' (Henry IV
Part 2 1.2.8–9). Hal goes on to become a master of rhetorical
manipulation, immortalised by Shakespeare in his St Crispin's
Day speech in Henry V.

A characteristic feature of their relationship is their trading of witty insults. Take, for instance, this exchange:

Prince: . . . This sanguine coward, this bed-presser, this
            horse-back-breaker, this huge hill of flesh—
Falstaff: 'Sblood, you starveling, you eel-skin, you dried
            meat's tongue, you bull's pizzle, you stock-fish! Oh,
            for breath to utter what is like thee, you tailor's yard,
            you sheath, you bow-case, you vile standing tuck—
                                    (*Henry IV Part 1* 2.4.221–227)

In an early modern version of locker room talk, both interlocutors trade bawdy comments, defining each other in sexual terms: 'bed-presser' refers to Falstaff's licentious habits, while the string of epithets that Falstaff unleashes are dripping with ribald innuendo, from 'bull's pizzle' (or penis), 'stock-fish' (dried cod), 'tailor's yard' (or measuring stick), 'sheath' and 'bow-case' (both punning on 'foreskin') to 'standing tuck' (an upright rapier). In retaliation for Hal's jibes at his enormous size, Falstaff pokes fun at Hal as skinny. His fertile fantasy takes flight with a hilarious series of riffs on thinness which double as images for Hal's sexual parts, deflating the prince by equating him with his penis. As in all joking relationships, Falstaff and Hal's slanging match combines play with one-upmanship, fellowship with aggression. In view of the underswell of hostility between them that runs through the play, their jesting is also a way of negotiating power relations, albeit under the cloak of wit.

WIT AND REPARTEE

The term 'wit' underwent a shift in meaning during the early modern period.[5] It was originally used to denote the intellectual and perceptive faculties. For several centuries, philosophers had drawn on Aristotelian conceptions of psychology, embellished by accretions of late classical and Arabic thought, and had distinguished between a range of 'inward' senses, which consisted of imagination, cogitation or instinct, fantasy, memory, and common sense, often referred to as 'the five wits', and the five 'external' senses of vision, hearing, smell, taste, and touch. These ten senses were seen as related, and while they were a mark of humankind, they were also partly shared by animals. Accordingly, they were regarded as subordinate to the intellect, with which only humans were endowed. By 1600, the theory of five separate internal senses had dissipated, and all five were generally collapsed into what most philosophers termed the imagination.[6] The term 'wit' could also, however, refer to reason and judgement, that is, the highest intellectual faculties human beings possessed. This older meaning regained prominence during the early modern period. And by the end of the sixteenth century, the term 'wit' was used to denote inventive brilliance or verbal ingenuity. Increasingly, the current meaning of wit—using words in a sparkling and amusing way—crept into the language of Shakespeare and his contemporaries. But the older meanings remained in circulation. More importantly, the uneasy relation between wit as referring merely to ingenuity, and wit as referring to discernment, reflected the fact that both imaginative and verbal artistry were also frequently denounced as frothy and meretricious. This was an age in which moralists frowned on attractive surfaces of any kind, be it images, ornament, or artifice, as a distraction from spiritual concerns and the works of God. The opposing ideas about the value of wit are often played out in the plays themselves. In this chapter, the focus is on the way Shakespeare's plays display witty jesting in social interaction—in scenarios that are remarkably evocative of contemporary society.

Shakespeare's drama, in particular the comedies, depicts a world in which not just the entertainer figures (fools or jesters) show off their verbal dexterity in a never-ending flow of smart quips, but in which an entire array of characters participate in battles of wit, firing off a barrage of brilliant rapid-fire remarks at each other. These are often the most attractive characters in the play, the bright young things engaged in endless rounds of pleasure, who 'fleet the time carelessly' in social games of friendly rivalry or love (or both).[7] A vogue for witty language swept Renaissance literature, propelled by the resurgence of rhetoric, propagated in the Humanist educational programme in the firm belief that wisdom and eloquence were closely interwoven. Writers like John Lyly launched a fashion for ingenious feats of language, one that was incessantly imitated and then parodied in the theatre.[8] Falstaff, a master at the game of all variations of wit, delivers a travesty of Euphuism when he and Hal stage 'a play extempore' (*1HIV* 2.4.255). Falstaff plays Hal's father and admonishes him for wasting his time with riff-raff like the Eastcheap gang, indulging in pastimes such as petty theft:

> Shall the blessed sun of heaven prove a micher [truant] and eat blackberries? A question not to be asked. Shall the son of England prove a thief and take purses? A question to be asked. . . . I do not speak to thee in drink but in tears; not in pleasure but in passion; not in words only but in woes also.
>
> (*Henry IV Part 1* 2.4.371–379)

Lyly's style of writing is marked by balance and antithesis, with clauses of parallel structure and a plethora of figures of speech like repetition, alliteration, and rhetorical questions. Falstaff has fun masquerading as the strait-laced king and lecturing his son in the gushing idiom of stylish courtiers, and sends up the Euphuistic mode in the bargain, churning out a sequence of apparent oppositions (not drink but tears, not pleasure but passion, not words but also woes) which are blatantly absurd. Is this 'king' insisting that his watery eyes are not the effect of alcohol but of true sorrow? A question not to be asked.

Not only is Falstaff scoffing at the king and the literary vogue of Euphuism—Shakespeare is mocking the wit of an earlier generation of writers. In the highly competitive early modern marketplace for print, playwrights were continually parodying each other, striving to draw attention to their own style as superior to that of their fellow writers. Competition and gamesmanship are always an inherent element in the use of wit. This is because wit was bound up with prestige: the wittier a person or a writer was, the more admiration they garnered. The differentiation of humour along a scale of status, and the high store set by verbal wit, is a characteristic feature of the Renaissance. It was not, however, a Renaissance invention, but was modelled on classical notions of humour.

In the Renaissance, one of the principal templates for witty speech stemmed from Cicero, whose *De oratore* describes wit as an indispensable accomplishment for the ideal orator. Humour is a useful resource in oratory for a number of reasons: to score points against one's opponent, to contribute to a relaxed atmosphere, and because 'it shows the orator himself to be refined, to be educated, to be well bred' (2.236).[9] It was Cicero too who set up a distinction that is still cited in discussions of humour. He divides witticisms into two kinds, amusing anecdotes, whose humour lies in content, and witty speech or verbal humour. While both can cause laughter, an orator must be careful to set himself off from buffoonish characters or professional mimes (at the time mime was not silent, but a vulgar form of drama). Sharp-witted one-liners are highly recommended as 'a sign of cleverness' (2.254). They might not have the audience rolling in the aisles, but they earn esteem for the speaker. In particular, orators should cultivate an aptitude for cutting retorts, which, unlike recycled jokes, give the appearance of spontaneity: 'in retort a greater quickness of mind is apparent' (2.230).

Of equal significance was the work of Quintilian, whose *Institutio Oratoria* only existed in fragments in the medieval period, but—in one of the most sensational recoveries of classical works in the Renaissance—was discovered by the Humanist scholar Poggio Bracciolini in 1416 while rummaging through the Swiss monastery of St Gall. Quintilian reiterates the points that Cicero makes; he too stresses the quality of repartee. In addition, he highlights the desirability of 'urbane' wit, a term that originally alluded to the type of pungent witticisms that marked someone as an inhabitant of Rome. As Quintilian notes, 'it is brevity that gives "urbane" wit more point and speed'.[10] Centuries later, these words would be turned into a joke by Shakespeare. In *Hamlet*, Polonius, a monumentally boring windbag, lectures his royal audience that 'brevity is the soul of wit' (*Ham.* 2.2.90)—before launching into yet another tedious speech.

HUMOUR AND SOCIAL DISTINCTION

The comments on humour by both Cicero and Quintilian had a decisive impact on Renaissance views of taste. Both classical writers point out that humour can be amusing without necessarily producing gales of laughter. Both draw a link between humour and class—coarse humour of the variety produced by uncouth individuals and professional entertainers was to be disdained. Prestige, on the other hand, could be acquired by means of quick-witted ripostes that give the appearance of being spontaneous, even if the ability to fire off a stinging retort has been carefully cultivated. And both writers call attention to wit as an urban phenomenon. These notions continue to hold sway in Renaissance modes of jesting, both in courtly circles and in urban life.

The influence of rhetoric is not only visible in the curricula of grammar schools and universities but was also formative in social life.[11] Cicero had written for a world that disappeared with the fall of the Roman Republic. No longer did persuasive rhetoric play a role in political life or in the process of law-making. In the medieval period, oratory dwindled into a discipline of arcane rules and schemes. All this changed in the Renaissance, when the Humanist love affair with the classical past began. Humanists used rhetoric to oust scholasticism from its pre-eminent position in the world of scholarship. With their emphasis on the active life, not merely spiritual concerns, and their conviction that eloquent speech was conducive to wisdom, they put rhetoric on the forefront of pedagogical and intellectual life. Although devotional texts dominated the book market, handbooks of rhetoric, self-help guides, and other educative works rolled off the printing presses in Europe too.[12] Some of them were originally earmarked for an elite audience, but once in print, were avidly seized upon and devoured by social aspirants of all stripes.

A genre whose titles were frequently intended rather to promote social exclusion than invite a wide readership to fashion themselves in accordance with their precepts was the courtesy book. One of most influential of these works was

Castiglione's Book of the Courtier (1528), translated into English by Sir Thomas Hoby in 1561. Castiglione based his work on Cicero's De oratore, with one important difference: he replaced the profession of the orator with that of the courtier. Under the guise of a series of sprightly conversations, the book promulgates rules of courtesy that are imperative for a courtier intent on carving out a career for himself at the new centres of power, the courts. By the fourteenth century, princely states had replaced most of the republican city-states in Italy. In the rest of Europe, feudal power bases were crumbling, and the focal points of political life in the emerging nation states were the royal courts.

The Book of the Courtier became a bestseller. By the early 1600s, around sixty-two editions had appeared in Italy, while a further sixty editions appeared in translations and adaptations, in Spanish, English, German, French, and Polish.[13] The book was not consumed by courtiers alone. One reason why it appealed to such a wide swathe of society was that its ideas were the stuff of the Renaissance, especially the crucial thought that human nature was not determined by birth, but malleable: 'man is certainly not born, but made man', as Erasmus famously put it.[14] Erasmus, an indefatigable propagandist of the benefit of education, was referring above all to our personality, but for his contemporaries, this was taken to have a bearing on one's position in society as well.

A raft of other courtesy books teaching its readers the rules of proper behaviour appeared in the wake of Castiglione's treatise, many of them plagiarised versions of The Courtier. For his part, Castiglione borrowed heavily from Cicero's section on humour. One of the four books of The Courtier focuses on the type of jokes a courtier should make. It brims over with jests, many of which, in a time-honoured ploy of the joke genre, were taken straight from Cicero's *De oratore*, but given a contemporary twist. An insight that *The Courtier* instilled into the minds of his contemporaries of all social strata was the notion that humour, like manners or dress, is a mode of self-presentation. You are defined by the type of jokes you crack. Style is a crucial factor that affects how we appear to others and largely determines social status. This observation still holds today: we are not only the clothes we wear, the food we eat, the cars we drive, and the books we read (or don't read), but also the jokes we make and what we find funny.[15] As humour theorists have shown, humour might be a trait of all human societies, but what we laugh about is specific to a certain culture and milieu.[16] But if this is true, the corollary would be that there is nothing that is intrinsically funny. Humour is a social practice: it is a society or a group that determines what is amusing or not. Their laughter *creates* the humour. What this also suggests is that we choose what we find funny—which has significant implications for the ethical import of humour.

Another concept that Castiglione popularised was the value of spontaneity. He coined the term *sprezzatura* for the air of nonchalance that the ideal courtiers should display in everything they say and do. Poise and insouciance became markers of membership in the club of the elite in the coming centuries and remain essential elements to attain cachet in many societies. *Sprezzatura* might, for instance, be compared to the concept of 'cool' in urban black culture. As Castiglione takes care to point out, however, the impression of casual ease that we should cultivate is produced by dint of hard work and assiduous practice. It is the appearance of spontaneity that counts, a simulation of effortlessness that carefully conceals the exertion necessary to achieve expertise in a certain field. Castiglione's book itself might be regarded as an exercise in *sprezzatura*. As might Shakespeare's plays, which rarely betray the labour invested into producing artistic masterpieces. It is also worth noting that *The Courtier* was addressed to both men and women. The English translation was advertised on its title page as 'very necessary and profitable for yonge Gentilmen and Gentlewomen abiding in Court, Palaice or Place'.[17] With the exception of Falstaff, Shakespeare's wittiest creations are his women. The next chapter will be devoted entirely to them.

Not everyone approved of the passion for stylish wit by which early modern society was consumed. In his *Scholemaster* (1570), the humanist Roger Ascham sets out an educational programme for the future members of the elite. Listing the qualities a young mind should possess, he distinguishes between 'quick' wits and 'hard' wits. It is clear that he is not referring solely to youths, but to his peers. 'Quick wits', he asserts, are those who display mental sharpness and cleverness, but whose refinement is a meretricious facade. 'Hard wits' are careful, conscientious, and labour assiduously to acquire virtue.[18] Cavils by Ascham and other thinkers remain as a dark undercurrent in debates about ethics and aesthetics in the period. But for those aspiring to burnish their social prestige, they were immaterial.

The observations about wit mooted by classical rhetoricians were transposed into recommendations about humour in social life by writers of courtesy books, Castiglione and his epigones. Decisive is the form of humour, not the content (which remained similar to that of earlier periods): urbane wit and swift ripostes are regarded as a sign of sophistication, skills it is imperative to finesse to achieve social distinction. Early modern English society was in the throes of a dream of upward mobility. Historians such as Lawrence Stone have pointed out that there was in fact a short period which saw an unprecedented surge in social mobility—the period between around 1540 and 1640. Stone bases his findings on a meticulous study of the sale of land—always associated with elite status in England—which reaches a peak in the first decade of the seventeenth century.[19] He attributes the upheaval on the land market to a number of factors, including the dissolution of monasteries under Henry VIII, commercial growth in a nascent market economy, and the large-scale creation of gentlemen under an impoverished James I, who was keen to tap into social aspiration as a much-needed source of income. What is of greater interest than the actual reality of upward mobility, which, however unusual for its time, might have been relatively limited in scope, is the fact that the society as a whole appears to share the fantasy of climbing up the social ladder. It is this fantasy that fuels so much of the drama of the period, be it set at court, in great houses, or in the metropolis.

If the early modern age witnessed a growth in courts, far more drastic was the expansion of urban centres. The explosion in the demographics of London was unprecedented, on a par with the development of cities like Mumbai in Asia or Sao Paolo in South America in the twentieth century. The size of the population of London increased almost ten-fold between 1500 and 1700. Urban audiences developed a taste for entertainment that celebrated the traits that were of vital importance in negotiating the obstacles of urban life: resourcefulness, audacity, a knack for improvisation, and a capacity for nimble-witted responses. The jokes that Castiglione lifted from Cicero (and that other writers lifted from him) were recycled in jestbooks. They moulded the type of humour Shakespeare and his peers aimed for. The English theatre of this period was, after all, a product of modernity, one that catered largely to an urban crowd who oscillated between deploring city life and priding themselves on their street credibility. Unlike most of his peers, Ben Jonson, Thomas Middleton, Thomas Heywood, John Marston, Thomas Dekker, and John Webster, Shakespeare barely contributed to the burgeoning new genre of city comedy. The only play of his occasionally categorised as a city comedy, The Merry Wives of Windsor, is set in the provincial town of Windsor, although admittedly the Henriad teems with urban scenes, mainly set at an Eastcheap tavern.[20] But Shakespeare had a sharp eye for the concerns that preoccupied his spectators. One of them is the desire to present oneself as adept at sharp-witted repartee to enhance one's social prestige, be it among one's peers or before an audience one strives to impress. In the plays, wit is by no means restricted to aristocratic characters. The early modern theatre absorbed the tradition of Roman New Comedy, which was thronged with witty servants and tricksters. Boosting one's status was a preoccupation at all levels of society, and accordingly, audiences were highly appreciative of witty repartee, ministering as it did to their sense of cultural sophistication.

WITTY JOUSTS

In the early comedy, The Two Gentlemen of Verona, a brace of characters engage in a tussle of wits that provides an opportunity to foreground their mastery of repartee for their audience: the lady whose hand both young men hope to win, and the spectators in the theatre. Valentine, newcomer to the court of the Duke of Milan, is competing for the love of Silvia, the Duke's daughter, with Turio, a cowardly and somewhat dull-witted gentleman of ample means, who, unfortunately for our hero, is favoured by Silvia's father. The witty servant of Valentine's, Speed, has a simple solution to the dilemma: ''Twere good you knocked him', he advises his master (2.4.7).

Largely thanks to Speed and Silvia, Valentine has picked up a smattering of cultivation since arriving at the Ducal court. Silvia returns his love, but social norms forbid her from expressing herself clearly. Instead, she asks him to write a love letter for her addressed to a 'secret nameless friend' (2.1.93), which, once he has fulfilled the task, she returns to him, using the ruse to make a coded declaration of love. Valentine is too obtuse to comprehend her meaning and offers to write another, compelling Silvia to be more explicit: 'when it's writ, for my sake read it over,/And if it please you, so' (116–117). Speed, on the other hand, observing the scene, immediately grasps the beauty of the manoeuvre, and applauds the 'jest unseen' (122) in an aside to the audience: 'Oh excellent device! Was there ever a better?' (126). He admires the subtle joke Silvia has played on her suitor and explains to the crest-fallen Valentine that by having him write a love letter to himself, she has taught him a lesson in the sophisticated art of wooing.[21]

The next time we encounter the protagonist, he has become more adroit in the refinements of jesting. Turio attempts to provoke him, but he rises to the occasion.

Silvia:	Servant, you are sad.[22]
Valentine:	Indeed, madam, I seem so.
Turio:	Seem you that you are not?
Valentine:	Haply I do.
Turio:	So do counterfeits.
Valentine:	So do you.
Turio:	What seem I that I am not?
Valentine:	Wise.
Turio:	What instance of the contrary?
Valentine:	Your folly.

Turio: And how quote you my folly?
Valentine: I quote it in your jerkin.

(2.4.8–19)

Turio and Valentine play out their rivalry for the favour of Silvia in a battle of words. Turio leads the attack, pouncing on the word 'seem' and twisting it to imply that Valentine is dissembling his love. Valentine neatly turns the tables on him, stating that Turio is shamming, too: the impression he makes of being a man of the world is a facade.[23] When Turio angrily clamours to be given proof of his lack of sophistication, Valentine cites the cut of his apparel. This is actually a hit below the belt, but Silvia is impressed. 'A fine volley of words, gentlemen, and quickly shot off' (31–32), she compliments her two suitors.

Ignoring Speed's suggestion to resort to violence, Valentine opts for a skirmish of repartee, using barbed wit as a weapon to best his opponent. His thrust at Turio's dress is intended to expose his rival as less adept not only in the artful feints and parries of witty speech, but also as deficient in the discipline of sartorial style. Deftly, he turns Silvia's remark into a counter-compliment, citing her as the source of inspiration for both parties. He nimbly combines the compliment with a sally at the expense of his rival, claiming 'Turio borrows his wit from your ladyship's looks' (36), insinuating he has no wit of his own. Unlike his loss of face in the scene with the letter, this time Valentine scores all around. To his mistress, he displays his virtuosity in the game of wit and love; to the audience, he demonstrates how to acquire social distinction through witty repartee.

Shakespeare's portrayal of jesting relationships would become increasingly multi-layered. In *Romeo and Juliet*, a tragedy that starts off as a comedy, we observe fashionable young bloods hanging around together, tossing jocular insults at one another and playing at being in love with women—until one of them actually falls in love with a woman. The tension between friendship amongst men and romantic love between men and women is, of course, a motif that runs through many of Shakespeare's plays. In *Romeo and Juliet*, this tension is briefly explored in a comic key, in a scene of jesting between Romeo and his friends, chief of whom is Mercutio, the wittiest character in the play.[24]

In one of the preceding scenes, Romeo has declared his love for Juliet and, as a proof of his serious intents, has agreed to get married. In Shakespeare's portrayal of two adolescent lovers, the initiative comes from Juliet, who takes the lead in their relationship throughout the play, foreshadowing the dynamics between couples such as Rosalind and Orlando in *As You Like It*, Olivia and Sebastian in *Twelfth Night*, and in a darker vein, between Lady Macbeth and Macbeth. Friar Laurence, whom Romeo seeks out to beg him to arrange a clandestine betrothal, upbraids him for his fickleness in love and reminds him of the histrionic passion he displayed for his previous love, Rosaline. The Friar finally agrees to a marriage between Romeo and Juliet, hoping to engineer a reconciliation between the warring families.

In response to the remonstrances of his confessor, all Romeo puts forward in his defence is the assertion that unlike Rosaline, Juliet shares his feelings, to which the Friar remarks caustically, 'she knew well/Thy love did read by rote, that could not spell' (2.2.87–88). Rosaline, he implies, has taken the measure of the callow youth; she has realised that, by analogy with someone who has learned a role by heart but is unable to read, Romeo was only going through the motions of love. *Romeo and Juliet* is often grouped together with other plays composed between 1594 and 1596 in Shakespeare's 'lyrical' period, *Love's Labour's Lost*, *Richard II*, and *A Midsummer Night's Dream* (which contains a parodic version of *Romeo and Juliet* in the play-within-a-play, 'Pyramus and Thisbe'). Perhaps the masquerade of love that the four lords stage for the benefit of the four ladies in *Love's Labour's Lost*, one of whom bears the same name as Romeo's first love, Rosaline, has left its traces on the depiction of Romeo. The impression lingers that being in love is a routine pastime for the aristocratic young man, merely a role he delights slipping into. There is no sign that this time things are different.

At all events, Mercutio has little reason to think so. Before Romeo appears, his friends discuss the letter that Tybalt has sent to old Montague, Romeo's father, and speculate whether it might be a challenge to a duel. As the friends might have observed, Tybalt recognised Romeo at the masked ball despite his visor, and is boiling with rage at the insolence of the Montague clique in insinuating themselves into the mansion of their mortal enemies under false pretences. While Benvolio is delighted at the thought of a duel between his cousin and their rivals, Mercutio mourns Romeo's preoccupation with the trivial affairs of the heart. 'Alas, poor Romeo, he is already dead—stabbed with a white wench's black eye, run through the ear with a love song' (2.3.13–15), he jibes. The words, however funny in the surreal image that they conjure up, resonate with unintended irony: it is Mercutio who will shortly be stabbed to death—not metaphorically, with the fatal look of a lady, but by Tybalt, when Mercutio later takes up the challenge on Romeo's behalf. For Mercutio, women inevitably kill the friendship between young men. In this regard too, his scoffing remarks are prescient: torn between divided loyalties,

Romeo declines to fight with Tybalt, his kinsman through marriage to Juliet.

When Romeo arrives on the scene, Mercutio jeers at him as emasculated and worn thin from too much wooing: 'Without his roe, like a dried herring! O flesh, flesh, how art thou fish-ified' (35–36). Characteristically, Mercutio's words sparkle with word-play and innuendo: 'roe' might glance at Rosaline, Romeo's love (Mercutio and Benvolio are not quite *au courant* with Romeo's latest venture in the field of love), without whom Romeo is only half his former self. In fact, what was once a man of flesh and blood has shrivelled up like a dried fish whose roe have been removed; the bawdy implications are patent. Alternatively, Mercutio indicates, without the first half of his name, all the remains of Romeo is a 'meow', a pussy-cat, who will never be in a position to stand up to the 'Prince of Cats' (18), as Mercutio has just dubbed Tybalt. He continues, taunting Romeo as a spouter of love poetry: 'Now is he for the numbers that Petrarch flowed in: Laura to his lady was a kitchen wench' (36–38), and goes on to debunk the celestial mistress of the *Canzoniere* by lining her up in the company of kitchen wenches and harlots. Interestingly, Shake-speare's only reference to Petrarch, the uncrowned prince of love poetry, comes in the form of a jest at the poet's expense. Mercutio ends his caricature of men in love by declaring: 'You gave us the counterfeit fairly last night' (42). His pun plays with the meanings of giving someone the slip and giving someone false money. But like Friar Laurence, Mercutio inti-mates that Romeo's passion is fraudulent: he is merely putting on a performance of being in love.

What we observe next is a different Romeo, or perhaps the old Romeo, who rises to the occasion with bravura and immediately engages in a dazzling verbal duel with Mercutio, in which each of them riffs off the ripostes of the other in a double act of equally virtuosic, superbly synchronised wits. At one point, Romeo gains the upper hand, and Mercutio gives up in feigned despair: 'Nay, if our wits run the wild goose chase, I am done; for thou hast more of the wild goose in one of thy wits than I am sure I have in my whole five' (65–67). He cannot keep up with Romeo's riotous fantasy, he declares. Romeo promptly picks up the word 'goose' and runs with it: 'Thou wast never with me for anything when thou wast not there for the goose' (69–70), he states flatly, turning Mercutio's allusion to a metaphorical goose, implying folly, into a bawdy reference to prostitutes (sometimes termed 'geese') and teasing his friend about his insatiable appetite for whores. Male banter about sex, as opposed to maudlin love talk, is fully to Mercutio's taste, who playfully threatens, 'I will bite thee by the ear for that jest', in response to which Romeo pleads in mock-terror, using a proverbial cry for mercy, 'Nay, good goose, bite not!' (71–72). The hint of sexual attraction between the two men is often picked up and developed in stage or film interpretations of the play.[25]

The jesting scenario in *Romeo and Juliet* is quite different to the one in *Two Gentlemen of Verona*. Quick, trenchant repartee is deployed as a weapon in both jousts of wit, but the rivalry between Romeo and Mercutio is inextricably entwined with companionship. Like Valentine and Turio, the two young Veronese gentlemen in the later play are vying for the prize of social acclamation for their verbal suppleness. In the earlier play, the goal is to win approbation from the lady they are wooing and the rest of the courtly company, in the later play, to earn kudos from the other members of their coterie, or simply from each other. Joking relationships are not only a conduit for power relations. They also create a sense of bonding amongst peers and cement a friendship. For many of Shakespeare's young men, jesting and trading insults is a competitive game into which antagonism within a group is deflected. Much of their humour is ribald, and targeted at women, against whom they close ranks. The content of the jests is, however, largely immaterial. The function these jokes fulfil is to shore up an ideal of an exclusively male (or alternatively, female) world, under threat from the opposite sex. Humour is a strategy of defence against those perceived as outsiders, and in the scenarios of the plays, a technique to defuse anxiety about betrayal by members of one's own circle. At the end of their bout of wit, Mercutio exclaims triumphantly, 'Why, is not this better now than groaning for love? Now art thou sociable; now art thou Romeo' (80–81). For a brief moment, Mercutio believes he has won back his old friend. The play proves him wrong.

MUCH ADO ABOUT JESTING

Shakespeare's most stylish play about jesting relationships is *Much Ado About Nothing*. Often termed the first comedy of manners, it paves the way for the crosstalk of Restoration comedy, in which plots exist mainly to showcase the effervescent wit of the protagonists. (In the most extreme variant of the genre, as in Oscar Wilde's *The Importance of Being Earnest*, plot disappears entirely, while the characters perform a stylised dance of social interplay which mockingly holds up a mirror to the audience and its values.) *Much Ado About Nothing* is, however, much richer than merely the portrayal of the mores of a set of smart young people. Among other things, it displays a range of jesting interactions between its protagonists, in which jokes are deployed as a tool of attack, as a means of winning social distinction, to facilitate bonding within a group, and to erect a bulwark against perceived threats to the cohesion of the group. In Shakespeare's comedies, many of these mechanisms are visible in male attempts to ward off the intrusion of women into their circle of friends. In *Much Ado About Nothing*, a seamless mutation from one mode into another is perceptible. In addition, jokes are pressed into service as a flirtation gambit.

In the discipline of jesting, the three gallants we encounter at the beginning of the play are evidently an experienced team. When Claudio breaks the news of his love for Hero to Prince Pedro, he is fully in earnest. But the group cannot resist slipping into their old comic routine:

Pedro: By my troth, I speak my thought.
Claudio: And in my faith, my lord, I spoke mine.
Benedict: And by my two faiths and troths, my lord, I spoke
                 mine.
Claudio: That I love her, I feel.
Pedro: That she is worthy, I know.
Benedict: That I neither feel how she should be loved, nor
                 know how she should be worthy, is the opinion that
                 fire cannot melt out of me. I will die in it at the stake.
                                                                                    (1.1.185–198)

Benedict, the lowest in rank, is by far superior to his peers in wit. He gives a comic twist to their words, scoffing at their pious sentiments and debunking their solemn statements by parroting them in absurd hyperbole ('two faiths and troths') or outright contradiction. A 'rule of three' is a standard formula in jokes, in which a build-up is required in order to increase the effect of the punchline. Benedict's running gag is his exaggerated horror at the thought of marriage, a belief, he proclaims, for which he is willing to be martyred. The jest of the play lies in gulling him into an apparent conversion, mainly to offer his more slow-witted companions an opportunity for once to trump him in the contest of wit. But in the first scene of the play, he is vociferous in his views. When Don Pedro warns him that one day he will come around to the notion of marriage, citing the proverbial wisdom, 'In time the savage bull doth bear the yoke' (221–222), Benedict retorts:

> The savage bull may, but if ever the sensible Benedict bear
> it, pluck off the bull's horns and set them in my forehead.
> And let me be vilely painted, and in such great letters as they
> write, 'Here is a good horse to hire', let them signify under
> my sign, 'Here you may see Benedict, the married man.'
>
> (1.1.223–228)

The hallmark of Benedict's wit is his bizarre fantasy and his penchant for piling one grotesque image on another. Not content to score by wrenching the adage into a literal description of a bull whose horns will be transplanted into his forehead, he spins out the conceit, demanding that a likeness of himself be painted and hung up in public, in the manner in which signs advertising horses are to be found before taverns. The entire flight of fancy is intended primarily to keep his friends amused and to bolster his own reputation as the wittiest man in Messina. Nothing wounds him more deeply than to hear himself sneered at as 'the Prince's jester' (2.1.122), a jab Beatrice lands during the masque. The idea of degrading him to the status of a professional entertainer is a profound blow to Benedict's pride, perhaps because it cuts too close to the bone.

Cuckoldry jokes are Benedict's speciality. They are a staple of early modern humour, both in the theatre and in jestbooks, and will be discussed in more detail in the coming chapter. At this point, suffice it to note that marriage, in Benedict's eyes, is inevitably bound up with female betrayal. His belief reflects a widespread anxiety in early modern society about insubordinate women, and the gnawing awareness, however unvoiced, that the ideology of patriarchy does not correlate to the reality of women's abilities, or, in Elizabethan England, to the reality of female power.[26] *Much Ado About Nothing* depicts an attempt to counter this threat in the vicious plan to slander Hero and humiliate her on her wedding day.[27] Jokes about cuckoldry might well be a comic device to manage male unease about women. Nonetheless, I would argue, the primary thrust of the jokes in the context of Shakespeare's comedies is less a concern with deriding women than with salvaging a male utopia from which women are banished. Lampooning female betrayal is a tactic to grapple with the fear of betrayal by members of one's circle. When hearing of his friend's plans for marriage, Benedict's clamorous lamentation suggests a sense of loss at the collapse of an idyllic, exclusively male companionship that recalls the sentiments of Mercutio: 'Is't come to this? In faith, hath not the world one man but he will wear his cap with suspicion? Shall I never see a bachelor of three-score again?' (1.1.162–164). His mock-despair, couched in typically drastic imagery, in this case depicting married men as invariably in need of a cap to hide their horns, serves above all to hide his own melancholy under the semblance of a jest.

Jesting in *Much Ado About Nothing* is not only a conduit for self-fashioning, masculine rivalry, and bonding. The play has become famous for the brilliance of the 'merry war' (50), as Leonato terms it, between Benedict and Beatrice, two protagonists both alike in wit, during whose exuberant verbal skirmishes sparks fly, delighting audiences from Shakespeare's times to the present. When Benedict enters the stage, he is so absorbed in his own wisecracks that he almost overlooks Beatrice. She promptly punctures his pride with the mordant remark, 'I wonder that you will still be talking, Signor Benedict. Nobody marks you' (94–95). The following sample offers a taste of their sparring. Benedict declares to Beatrice that he has little interest in women. She responds with further deflationary wit and assures him she fully shares his feelings:

Beatrice: A dear happiness to women; they would else have been troubled with a pernicious suitor. I thank God and my cold blood, I am of your humour for that. I had rather hear my dog bark at a crow than a man swear he loves me.

Benedict: God keep your ladyship still in that mind. So some gentleman or other shall scape a predestinate scratched face.

Beatrice: Scratching could not make it worse, an 'twere such a face as yours were.

Benedict: Well, you are a rare parrot teacher.

Beatrice: A bird of my tongue is better than a beast of yours.

(1.1.104–114)

In a rapid-fire exchange, in which Beatrice applauds Benedict's abstention from wooing as good news for women, and Benedict congratulates his sex for their narrow escape at her hands, both parties swap ingenious insults at a breathless pace, with each antagonist flaunting their verbal artistry while seeking to outdo the other. The flyting match continues with disparaging remarks about Benedict's appearance and Beatrice's lack of originality, to descend into the imagery of a bestiary. When Benedict insinuates that like someone teaching a parrot the same stock phrases, Beatrice has only an impoverished store at her disposal, she counters by lauding the loquacity of a parrot over the muteness of a beast, a slur suggesting Benedict's deficiency in eloquence. The invective is stinging—both protagonists pride themselves on their wit—and, paradoxically, a back-handed tribute to the other as a worthy antagonist. For all their feats of one-upmanship, the encounter between these two charismatic characters sizzles with mutual attraction. In this play, competitive jesting can also serve as a technique of seduction. Beatrice and Benedict have clearly gone out of their way to engage each other in a game in which they lob ever more imaginative insults at the other. The dynamics between Beatrice and Benedict has inspired countless imitations in romantic comedy, in the theatre as well as in film: it has been a formative influence on the genre of screwball comedy. A latter-day revival of the formula of sparring antagonists who transmute into lovers is to be found in the film *Intolerable Cruelty*, directed by the Coen brothers.[28]

The film treats the love-hate relationship between a cutthroat divorce lawyer, Miles Massey (played by George Clooney) and the predatory fortune hunter, Marilyn Rexroth (played by Catherine Zeta-Jones). Early in the film, Miles invites the glamorous Marilyn, whose husband, Rex, he is representing, for dinner (Figure 1.2). Their dialogue is larded with a mixture of mutual allure and menace. Significantly, both resort to Shakespeare to score points over the other. Quoting Shakespeare in twenty-first-century courtship is, after all, a coded way of signalling social distinction, advertising the speaker as a man or woman of cultivated taste and throwing down the gauntlet to one's counterpart to lay bare their own cultural credentials. At the same time, the lines they cite, taken from Shakespearean love discourse, are a veiled amorous invitation: Marilyn cites lines by Adonis from *Venus and Adonis*, ostensibly to ward

Figure 1.2 *Intolerable Cruelty* (2003), Dir. Ethan Coen, Joel Coen, produced by Universal Pictures, Imagine Entertainment (present), Alphaville Films (in association with) (as Alphaville), Mike Zoss Productions

off Miles' attempt at flirtation, while Miles cites Shakespeare's tribute to Marlowe's *Hero and Leander* in *As You Like It*, 'Who ever loved that loved not at first sight?' (3.5.819).

The duel of words see-saws between the antagonists, both ruthless players in their own sphere, with artful remarks ricocheting back and forth. At one point, Miles attempts to wrest control over the situation. He orders dinner for them both (tournedos of beef) without consulting Marilyn and asks her mockingly, 'I assume you are a carnivore?' Marilyn laughs disarmingly. When Miles embarks on conventional pick-up lines ('Tell me more about yourself'), she retaliates. 'Let me tell you everything you need to know. You may think you are tough, but I eat men like you for breakfast', she purrs. She then elaborates:

> I've invested five good years in my marriage to Rex and
> I've nailed his ass fair and square. Now I'm going to have it

stuffed, mounted, and have my lady friends come over and throw darts at it.

There is a remarkable resonance between Marilyn's words and similar lines in *Much Ado About Nothing*. Benedict, resentful of Beatrice's prowess in jesting, complains to Don Pedro about her. She is so sharp-witted that he feels under attack, he laments, smothered by her piling up 'jest upon jest with such impossible conveyance [or transmission, hence speed] upon me that I stood like a man at a mark with a whole army shooting at me'. He continues the analogy with another image from the language of weaponry: 'She speaks poniards [daggers] and every word stabs' (2.1.218–220). Whether in love or warfare, both Marilyn and Beatrice display effortless mastery of the arsenal of jests at their disposal in the perennial battle of the sexes.

NOTES

1 *Gran Torino*, dir. Clint Eastwood, perf. Clint Eastwood, Bee Vang, Ahney Her (Village Roadshow Pictures, Media Magik Entertainment, and Malpaso Productions, 2008).

2 A. R. Radcliffe-Brown, 'On Joking Relationships', *Journal of the International African Institute* 13.3 (July, 1940): 195–210. Also see Mahadev L. Apte, *Humor and Laughter: An Anthropological Approach* (Ithaca, NY: Cornell University Press, 1985), 29–66.

3 On early modern carnival practices see, inter alia, the seminal works of Peter Burke, *Popular Culture in Early Modern Europe*, 3rd ed. (London: Routledge, 2009), 255–86, and Natalie Zemon Davis, *Society and Culture in Early Modern France* (Stanford, CA: Stanford University Press, 1975), 97–123.

4 See C. L. Barber, *Shakespeare's Festive Comedy: A Study of Dramatic Form and Its Relation to Social Custom* (Princeton, NJ: Princeton University Press, 1959), Michael D. Bristol, *Carnival and Theater: Plebeian Culture and the Structure of Authority in Renaissance England* (New York: Methuen, 1985), and François

Laroque, *Shakespeare's Festive World: Elizabethan Seasonal Entertainment and the Professional Stage* (Cambridge: Cambridge University Press, 1991).

5 See 'wit, n.', *Oxford English Dictionary Online*. Also see Leo Salingar, '"Wit" in Jacobean Comedy', in *Dramatic Form in Shakespeare and the Jacobeans* (Cambridge: Cambridge University Press, 1986), 140–52, and Ian Munro, 'The Matter of Wit and the Early Modern Stage', in *A New Companion to Renaissance Drama*, ed. Arthur F. Kinney and Thomas Warren Hopper (Oxford: Wiley Blackwell, 2017), 513–28.

6 Aristotelian psychology distinguished between three gradations of the soul, the 'vegetative soul', the only soul that plants possessed, the 'sensitive soul', which, together with the 'vegetative soul', were (at least partially) possessed by animals, and the 'intellective soul'. The ten senses were regarded as part of the 'sensitive soul', while the purely rational faculties were grouped together as part of the 'intellective soul'. Only human beings were animated by all three kinds of soul. See Katharine Park, 'The Organic Soul', in *The Cambridge History of Renaissance Philosophy*, ed. Charles B. Schmitt and Quentin Skinner (Cambridge: Cambridge University Press, 1988), 464–84, on whom I draw in this section.

7 *As You Like It*, 1.1.103.

8 The term 'Euphuism' for the style of highly artificial prose that Lyly invented was taken from the title of his prose romance, *Euphues: The Anatomy of Wit* (1578), which was very popular in court circles. Lyly himself adopts the name of his protagonist, Euphues, from Roger Ascham's *The Scholemaster* (1570), who borrows the term from Plato's *Republic*. Plato lists intellectual keenness (or 'euphues') as a key criterion for the selection of youths as future rulers. See Plato, *The Republic*, trans. Desmond Lee, Penguin Classics (London: Penguin Books, 1987), 535b.

9 The section on wit runs from 2.216b to 2.290.

10 Quintilian, *The Orator's Education*, trans. Donald A. Russell, Loeb Classical Library (Harvard, MA: Harvard University Press, 2001), 6.3.45. Chapter 3 of Book 6 focuses exclusively on humour. On Roman humour, see Mary Beard, *Laughter in Ancient Rome: On Joking, Tickling, and Cracking Up* (Berkeley: University of California Press, 2014).

11 For a magisterial overview of rhetoric in the Renaissance, see both Brian Vickers, *In Defence of Rhetoric* (Oxford: Oxford University Press, 1988) and Peter Mack, *A History of Renaissance Rhetoric 1380–1620* (Oxford: Oxford University Press, 2011).

12 See Alan B. Farmer and Zachary Lesser, 'What Is Print Popularity? A Map of the Elizabethan Book Trade', in *The Elizabethan Top Ten: Defining Print Popularity in Early Modern England*, ed. Andy Kesson and Emma Smith (Farnham: Ashgate, 2013), 19–54.

13 See Peter Burke, *The Fortunes of the Courtier* (University Park, PA: The Pennsylvania State University Press, 1995), 41; 62.

14 Erasmus, *A Declamation on the Subject of Early Liberal Education for Children*, trans. Beert C. Verstraete, *Collected Works of Erasmus: Literary and Educational Writings 3 and 4*, Vol. 26, ed. J. K. Sowards (Toronto: University of Toronto Press, 1985), 291–346; 304.

15 The scholar whose groundbreaking work confirmed that Castiglione was right is the sociologist Pierre Bourdieu, whose *Distinction: A Social Critique of the Judgement of Taste*, trans. Richard Nice (1979; Cambridge, MA: Harvard University Press, 1984) discusses the role that taste plays in determining social status.

16 One of the most recent books to sum up the current theories of humour is Noel Carroll, *Humour: A Very Short Introduction* (Oxford: Oxford University Press, 2014). An overview of other works on humour is given at the end of the book.

17 *The courtyer of Count Baldessar Castilio divided into foure bookes*, trans. Thomas Hoby (1561), B1r.

18 Roger Ascham, *The Schoolmaster*, ed. Lawrence V. Ryan (1570; Ithaca, NY: Cornell University Press, 1967), 27.

19 He detects a rise of 250% in comparison to land sale statistics in the 1560s. See Lawrence Stone, 'Social Mobility in England, 1500–1700', *Past and Present* 33 (1966): 16–55, and his *The Crisis of the Aristocracy 1558–1641* (Oxford: Oxford University Press, 1965). Also see Keith Wrightson, *English Society, 1580–1680* (London: Routledge, 2003) and Keith Thomas, *The Ends of Life: Roads to Fulfilment in Early Modern England* (Oxford: Oxford University Press, 2009).

20 Martin Wiggins associates the shift in style identified with city comedy with the 'comedy of humours', a genre that derives its humour from exposing human quirks (which the Elizabethans termed 'humours'), pioneered by George Chapman in *A Humorous Day's Mirth* (1597). Wiggins regards *The Merry Wives of Windsor* as Shakespeare's response to Chapman's innovations. See Martin Wiggins, *Shakespeare and the Drama of His Time*, Oxford Shakespeare Topics (Oxford: Oxford University Press, 2000), 64–78.

21 For a discussion of the play as an exploration of the mores of courtly society, see Camille Wells Slights, 'Common Courtesy in *The Two Gentlemen of Verona*', in *Shakespeare's Comic Commonwealths* (Toronto: University of Toronto Press, 1993), 57–73.

22 In courtly love discourse, servant referred to a lover.

23 'Wise' could mean being well-informed and knowledgeable. See 'wise, adj.' 3a and b, *Oxford English Dictionary Online*.

24 On Mercutio, see especially Joseph A. Porter, *Shakespeare's Mercutio: His History and Drama* (Chapel Hill, NC: University of North Carolina Press, 1988).

25 An example is the filmed version, *William Shakespeare's Romeo + Juliet*, dir. Baz Luhrmann, perf. Leonardo DiCaprio, Claires Danes (Bazmark Productions, 1996), in which Mercutio, played by Harold Perrineau, appears in the ball scene as a drag queen whose relationship with Romeo has erotic overtones.

26 See Louis Montrose, *The Purpose of Playing: Shakespeare and the Cultural Politics of the Elizabethan Theatre* (Chicago: University of Chicago Press, 1996).

27 On the gender politics of the play, see in particular Carol Cook, '"The Sign and Semblance of Her Honor": Reading Gender Difference in *Much Ado About Nothing*', in *Shakespeare and Gender: A History*, ed. Deborah Barker and Ivo Kamps (New York: Verso, 1995), 75–103, and S. R. Cerasano, 'Half a Dozen Dangerous Words', in *Much Ado About Nothing and The Taming of the Shrew: Contemporary Critical Essays*, New Casebooks, ed. Marion Wynne-Davis (Basingstoke: Palgrave Macmillan, 2001), 31–50.

28 *Intolerable Cruelty*, dir. Joel and Ethan Coen, perf. George Clooney, Catherine Zeta-Jones (Imagine Entertainment, 2003).

Two

'Make doors upon a woman's wit, and it will out at the casement'
As You Like It 4.1.141–142

It is a truth universally acknowledged that women don't have a sense of humour. The legendary twentieth-century actress, manager, and director, Mrs Patrick Campbell, explains why this is the case. Turning to a tedious dinner partner, she allegedly said, 'Do you know why the Lord withheld the sense of humour from women? . . . That we may love you instead of laughing at you.'[1]

Humour researchers have indeed detected differences between men and women in the sphere of humour. Some scholars claim that female humour is more empathetic and concerned with interrelationships between people, while male humour is aggressive and combative.[2] A recent study by the sociologist Giselinde Kuipers based on fieldwork in the Netherlands comes to a similar conclusion.[3] Women, she contends, do not employ less humour in social situations, but they use it differently. The female style of humour is more cooperative, while male humour is more competitive; women use humour to create solidarity, men to establish dominance. Kuipers' research focuses on the genre of the joke and the settings in which jokes are bandied about: pubs, social gatherings, and parties. In other words, she looks at the performative contexts in which

DOI: 10.4324/9780429317507-3

jokes are traded and notes that the discipline of joke-telling is a male-dominated one. She attributes this to the fact that making a joke always involves an element of risk. The dividends are large—gaining a reputation for being entertaining accrues significant cultural capital—but the risk of losing face if the joke falls flat is not negligible. For women, the dangers of social exposure are far greater than for men. A whiff of attention-seeking always lingers about women who crack jokes successfully, while a quip that fizzles out like a damp squib entails a higher price for women than for men in terms of derision and loss of countenance, since women need to invest considerable labour into wresting the limelight from men. Raunchy jokes are even more fraught, since they invite the impression that the joke-maker (if a woman) is obsessed with sex.

Paradoxically, Kuipers discovered that when questioned separately about their taste in humour, a remarkable correlation between male and female interviewees is discernible. Men and women laugh about precisely the same things, it appears, although men insist that certain type of jokes are ones women would reject as either too malicious or too embarrassing. What this suggests is that rather than the existence of an innate difference between male and female humour, what is crucial are role expectations and the performative situation in which joking takes place. Jokes are displays of social authority. Making jokes is a masculine way of establishing control over a social scenario. Laughing at jokes, on the other hand, is a demonstration of traits associated with conventional femininity: compliance, a willingness to accommodate to others, and appreciation of male prowess. Like all performances, these patterns require continual reiteration to become cemented in social interaction.[4]

This is borne out by findings in a scientific study by one of the leading experts on laughter, the neuroscientist Robert

Provine.[5] In assessing his data, he found that women laugh more than men. Men, on the other hand, score highest at eliciting laughter. This, he notes, also holds true for other power relations, for instance, in staff meetings with professional colleagues: junior staff members were the most enthusiastic laughers, while most of the jokes were delivered by senior colleagues. Provine draws the conclusion that laughter is not predominantly about humour. It is about relationships.

A wind of change has swept over gender definitions since Shakespeare's age. From being creatures who, as early moderns believed, thought about nothing else but sex, talked incessantly about sex, and were generally unreliable specimens of humankind, women changed into paragons of virtue who blushed at the sight of piano legs and closed their eyes and thought of England while men went about their business.[6] According to historians such as Anthony Fletcher, the reversal in gender roles is linked to the scientific revolution and the gradual discarding of the humoral theory in the natural sciences.[7] The early modern period had inherited the Galenic physiology from antiquity, according to which gender was determined by the balance of humours in the body. Women were considered to have less heat and more moisture than men. Heat, however, was the most important element in the human constitution. In his *Generation of Animals*, Aristotle declares that women are imperfect men, paving the way for the received wisdom of generations of scholars.[8] Since women are less endowed with reason than men, they are less able to control their passions. When the humoral theory was discredited—the death blow was probably dealt by William Harvey's discovery of the systematic circulation of blood, published in a treatise in 1628—the idea that men and women were entirely distinct from each other took root.

As Fletcher observes, the biological differences that distinguished women from men were associated with a discrete female nature: compassion and empathy were now regarded as hallmarks of the feminine nature. These views have been so persuasive that they are ingrained in the fabric of popular belief in our own time. In the Shakespeare sitcom, *Upstart Crow*, Kate, Shakespeare's landlord's daughter, begs him for the chance to audition for a part in a play, disguised as a boy actor. Will Shakespeare warns her to avoid the key giveaway that she is woman: talking about her feelings. When the bemused Kate asks what men talk about, if not their feelings, the crisp answer is 'sex, beer, and sport'.[9]

While the early moderns saw women as sexually voracious, whose appetite was insatiable, by the end of the eighteenth century, a new paradigm was in place. Women were desexualised beings, whose moral sensibility was grounded in their anatomy. Scholars such as Nancy Cott have laid bare the fact the women too availed themselves of the image of women as more virtuous than men for their own ends, harnessing the notion that women are moral agents as a source of power. The ideology of women's moral superiority allowed them to carve out an arena of authority for themselves, both in the domestic sphere and in society in general, albeit at the price of a denial of female desire.[10] By contrast, women throughout history whose ambitions for power were more expansive in scope, from Cleopatra to Indira Gandhi to Angela Merkel, have set little store by a reputation for virtue.

A further reason why women were stigmatised as humourless is the steep rise in stock of humour since Shakespeare's time.[11] The entrenched equation of humour with ridicule only changed about a century after Shakespeare's death, when thinkers of the Scottish Enlightenment, in particular Francis

Hutcheson, redefined humour as benevolent and playful, not derisive. Increasingly, eighteenth-century thinkers, influenced by the writings of the Earl of Shaftesbury, who believed that human nature was guided by an intuitive sense of morality, reclaimed humour as a sign of sympathetic companionship with other members of society. Humour became a good thing; possessing a sense of humour became increasingly indispensable in all sectors of life, both professional and private. It invaded the realm of politics, too: from the mid-twentieth century, scripted zingers became a standard ploy for every politician on the campaign trail. Once humour became desirable, it became a male domain; women were branded as lacking a sense of humour.

Nonetheless, there has always been a vibrant tradition of female comedy. The recent past has seen a large crop of star female comics, ranging from Sarah Silverman to Tiffany Haddish to Amy Schumer to Hannah Gadsby. In countries like India, with a wealth of traditional comic modes, a new generation of professional women comedians has emerged among the English-speaking, metropolitan elite, reflecting the panoply of humour in a society where staunchly conservative segments of society jostle with a modern urban population. These performers have challenged the notion that women cannot make jokes, and that there is an inherent difference between male and female humour. They may or may not address different concerns than their male colleagues, but their jokes are every bit as aggressive, mordant, and vulgar—and as funny. The rise in confidence among female comics allows them to tilt at aspects of feminism, too. Michelle Wolf, for instance, takes a jab at the women's movement for equal rights (Figure 2.1). Dissecting what she terms the 'air-conditioned oppression' of privileged white women, she jokes, 'We were like, "We want jobs!" And then black women were like, "We have those! In your house! We're

NETFLIX

Figure 2.1 *Michelle Wolf: Joke Show* (2019), Dir. Lance Bangs, produced by Irwin Entertainment

working for you right now!" . . . Then we were like, "This is really confusing. Plus, the baby's crying. Can you go do that?'"[12]

In this chapter, a brief look at jestbooks and contemporary comedians reveals a rich seam of female humour that Shakespeare's plays mine. His female characters are in command of an entire repertoire of wit, much of it risqué humour. Some characters, like Cleopatra, use wit to heighten their seductive appeal and forge a reputation for themselves as both beautiful and clever. Others, like Mistress Page and Mistress Ford in *The Merry Wives of Windsor*, make a point of stressing that a woman can be witty without being wanton. And some characters, like Beatrice in *Much Ado About Nothing* or Rosalind in *As You Like It*, resort to humour as a flirtation device as well as an instrument to manage their fears and insecurity.

CLEOPATRA AND HEROIC DEFLATION

In early modern moral precepts about women, a triad of injunctions is continually rehearsed: women should be chaste, silent, and obedient. It was a truism that the three concepts were closely interrelated. In conversation with men, women were to demonstrate modesty and sobriety. Laughing and jesting were a mark of levity, if not worse; since women's mouths were conflated with their sexuality, excessive speech and boisterous laughter were an index of their sexual appetite.[13] Juan Luis Vives, the humanist scholar and educationalist who served as tutor to Princess Mary, daughter of Henry VIII, wrote an influential guidebook for women which was translated from the original Latin into English in 1529 and titled *Instruction of a Christian Woman*. It was very popular throughout the century. Vives explicitly links laughter to sex: laughing, he contends, is 'a sign of a verye light and dissolute minde'.[14] Exhorting women to beware of the signals that their mirth would send, he writes, 'if thou laugh when any man laugheth, though thou do it not of purpose, strayght they will say thou hast a fantasie unto the man and his sayinges, and there it were no great maistery to winne thee'.[15] In the eyes of society, he asserts, pleasure in jesting with the opposite sex is decoded as loose morals. His assessment chimes with ideas that endure to the present.

Curiously, or perhaps not, women were also expected to be entertaining to their menfolk. Vives recommends that wives keep a store of humorous (but not indecent) stories to cheer up their care-worn husbands: 'A wise woman should have in minde mery tales, and histories (howe bee it yet honest) wherewith she may refreshe her husband, and make him merry when he is weary.'[16] These contradictory notions remained in circulation throughout the early modern period. In one of the first English courtesy books addressed specifically to women, Richard Brathwait reminds his readers in Delphic terms that 'Silence in a Woman is a moving Rhetoricke, winning most, when in words it wooeth least.' At

Women and wit 55

the same time, he lauds women whose jests are 'savoury, yet without saltnesse'.[17] Silent spouses might have been models of rectitude but, as early modern men seem to have noticed, they were uninspiring company.

Early modern literature abounds in witty women, be it on stage or in print. Admittedly, they were often associated with promiscuity.[18] What is striking about Shakespeare's plays is that they ride rough-shod over the identification of silence with chastity and jesting with lasciviousness. They are brimful of witty women, some of whom are chaste and others who are not. Cleopatra, for instance, the quintessence of seduction, displays a fine line in biting wit that leaves Antony floundering. In grandiloquent rhetoric, Antony boasts about the magnitude of his love, first in financial terms and then even more expansively, in bombastic cosmic imagery. 'There's beggary in the love than can be reckoned', he brags, and adds that to delimit their love, Cleopatra would have to 'find out new heaven, new earth' (*Antony and Cleopatra* 1.1.15; 17). At this very moment a messenger enters with a letter from Rome, a world that Antony would prefer to ignore. In a barb that foreshadows the demolition of heroic glamour that the entire play enacts, Cleopatra taunts him about their probable contents.[19] She speculates mockingly: 'Fulvia perchance is angry. Or, who knows/If the scarce-bearded Caesar have not sent/His powerful mandate to you: "Do this, or this;/Take in that kingdom, and enfranchise that!"' (21–24). Antony, she insinuates, is anything but the shining hero he takes himself for. He is a pawn in the manoeuvres of his wife Fulvia, a power player with the best, and of his arch-rival Octavius Caesar. Nothing punctures Antony's heroic delusions more effectively than the suggestion that he is merely a cat's paw in Caesar's imperial plans.

To be sure, Cleopatra too indulges in burnishing the image of Antony for her own purposes, preferably when he is dead. In her eloquent eulogy, she compares him to a Colossus: 'His legs bestrid the ocean; his reared arm/Crested the world' (5.2.81–82). Yet throughout the play, she remains supremely in control of her performance. This is epitomised in her suicide, staged as a grand operatic spectacle, in stark contrast to Antony's bungled affair. For the audience, who usually had at least a smattering of classical lore, her tribute to Antony would contain an ironic sting: the colossal statue of Apollo that was reported to have straddled the harbour of Rhodes, erected to celebrate a famous military victory, collapsed only a few decades after being constructed.

As with the other witty heroines, Cleopatra's wit is not in opposition to her allure, but enriches it. Although generally less enthusiastic about the Egyptian queen than Shakespeare, Plutarch too draws attention to her powers of speech.

> Now her beawtie (as it is reported) was not so passing, as unmatchable of other women, nor yet suche, as upon present viewe did enamor men with her: but so sweete was her companie and conversacion, that a man could not possiblie but be taken. And besides her beawtie, the good grace she had to talke and discourse, her curteous nature that tempered her words and dedes was a spurre that pricked to the quick.[20]

What captivates Antony is not her beauty alone, but her company ('conversation' could refer to social behaviour in general as well as discourse). The main weapon of seduction in her arsenal is her refined and urbane conversation. Both in Shakespeare's play and in his source, Cleopatra uses wit as a device to enhance her reputation as the cynosure of sophistication.

In a passage that Shakespeare plundered almost verbatim from Thomas North's version of the *Life of Marcus Antonius*, the Greek biographer describes her legendary boat trip on the river of Cydnus. Plutarch's narrative continues with Cleopatra's invitation to Antony to dine with her, from which he returns bedazzled by her sumptuous lifestyle. Attempting to compete, he returns the invitation the following evening, only to realise that she outstrips him in magnificence by far. Her superiority manifests itself not only in a more opulent way of life, but also in terms of wit. Plutarch writes, 'And when Cleopatra found Antonius jeasts and slents to be but grosse, and souldier like, in plaine manner: she gave him finely, and without feare taunted him throughly.'[21] In the rivalry that shadows the passion of these two immeasurably self-absorbed personalities, Cleopatra far exceeds Antony in elegance and style. The contrast between them embodies the antithetical appeal of the two cultural worlds that structures the play. In one of Cleopatra's wittiest remarks, she sums up the competing impulses that exert a fascination on Antony. Commenting on his sudden absence, she quips, 'He was disposed to mirth, but on the sudden/A Roman thought hath struck him' (1.2.80–81). Her acerbic witticism encapsulates the opposing forces of pleasure, decadence, and sensuality that life in Egypt represents and the ethos of masculine self-control propagated in Roman ideology. The play, however, proceeds to dismantle the tidy opposition she sets up. It emerges that for all their cultural differences, what both protagonists share is an insatiable hunger for power.

JESTING AND CUCKOLDRY

Early modern culture was awash with jokes about cuckoldry. Few jokes appear more tedious to us today, but judging by the number of cuckoldry jests in ballads, jestbooks, jigs, and plays, early moderns seem to have had a voracious appetite for them. Cultural critics who have scrutinised the jests claim that they shed light on the tensions within Renaissance society. On the cusp between the preindustrial age and modernity, the social world of the time was in the throes of radical upheaval. As has frequently been the case in times of turmoil throughout the world, a culprit was identified in women who were accused of having broken with tradition and upended societal norms.[22] These critics assert that jokes about unruly women are a form of gender control in the realm of fiction, holding out the warning of chastisement through laughter, much as real women were disciplined by the threat of drastic punishments such as the ducking stool, a chair to which disorderly women were tied and which was plunged into water, or the scold's bridle, an iron muzzle imposed on women accused of nagging.

It is true that one of the functions of jokes is to disseminate social information within a community and thus reinforce group norms. By mocking women as inevitably lascivious and untrustworthy, the jokes inculcate the message that to avoid being shamed, women need to safeguard their chastity. What considerably complicates the idea of cuckoldry jests as a conduit of social discipline, however, is the very nature of humorous discourse. A potential for ambiguity lurks within all discourse, but humour thrives on it: the essence of humour is ambiguity. Every joke depends on double meanings, building up an expectation about how it will unfold only for the punch line to pull the rug from under one's feet. Furthermore, different segments of an audience might find something funny for different reasons, even if they are laughing at the same joke. As regards cuckoldry jokes, a critic has argued recently that the jokes were as much about men ridiculing other men as about policing women.[23] The largest sector of consumers of cheap print were young men, whether apprentices or law students, who were under the sway of older, married men. They relished nothing so much as seeing patriarchal figures of authority humiliated by their wives. For their part, women might have appreciated cuckoldry jokes for quite different reasons. They might have enjoyed seeing the tables turned on domineering and suspicious husbands. Rather than absorbing the implicit didactic exhortations about pitfalls to avoid, they might have noted the witty ripostes of the jestbook characters as inspirational scripts.[24] For what is striking about the jests is how frequently they depict scenarios in which female protagonists vastly outdo their menfolk in wit and invite audience pleasure and admiration at their clever retorts.

A typical jest plot consists of the attempt of a husband to expose his wife as guilty of having cuckolded him. In the following example, taken from the first English jestbook, *A Hundred Merry Tales* (1526), the husband tries to trick his spouse into admitting her culpability by leading the way with an oath. When she counters with an oath in support of her innocence, he doubles back in order to pin her down. Nonetheless, she outwits him at every turn:

> The husband said to his wife thus wise: 'By this candle, I dreamed this night that I was a cuckold!'
>
> To whom she answered and said, 'Husband, by this bread, ye are none!'
>
> Then said he, 'Wife, eat the bread.'
>
> She answered and said to her husband, 'Then eat you the candle, for you swore first.'

By this a man may see that a woman's answer is never to seek.[25]

Early modern jestbooks were not mere repositories of oral culture, but they were written by humanists with a sharp sense for the richness and volatility of language, exploiting ambiguities and logical fallacies for comic capital. The deceptively simple form of the jokes is actually carefully crafted and based on precepts set out by Cicero in his description of the plain style in the *Orator*.[26] On one level, the joke lies in a linguistic game with figurative and literal meaning: the husband tries to ensnare his wife by suddenly shifting from the former to the latter. She counters by doing the same with his own oath, literally forcing him to eat his words. The moral tag that so many early modern jests append to the joke is itself less didactic than might appear at first sight. This one appears attached to three different jests in the collection. The lesson it propagates is not, as one might expect, that women are unreliable, but that it is never a good idea to argue with them. It might be read as a tongue-in-cheek recommendation to capitulate to the superior wit of women.

The jest is unusual for its brevity. More frequently, earlier examples of jests are closer to medieval *exempla*, anecdotes with a moral point, than one-liners. In the course of the sixteenth century, the form changed: moral tags went out of fashion, and jests became shorter and snappier. They now appeared in collections authored by professional writers, such as the prolific hack John Taylor, a former waterman on the Thames who dubbed himself the Water Poet. But in this example from a century later, the woman in the jest still upstages the man.

A Company of neighbours that dwelt all in one rowe in one side of a street, one of them said: Let us be merry, for it is reported that we are all Cuckolds that dwell on our side of the street (except one). One of the women sate musing, to whom her husband said: wife, what, all *amort* [pensive]? Why art thou so sad? no, quoth shee, I am not sad, but I am studying which of our neighbours it is that is not a Cuckold.[27]

The humour lies in the way the wife coolly deflates the complacency of the husband, who seems to assume he is the exception to the rule that every single man in the street has been cuckolded by their wife, without explicitly admitting her guilt. Once again, the wife wins the battle of the sexes hands down. The joke also slyly pokes fun at the self-congratulatory pleasure men take in cuckoldry jokes, always presuming that cuckolds are other people.

JESTING WIVES

The thumbnail characterisation of the husbands in cuckoldry jests ranges from the scheming and the smug, as in these two examples, to the violent and the vicious. Men obsessed with cuckoldry, unlike the easy-going neighbour in the joke above, were termed 'horn-mad'. In *The Merry Wives of Windsor*, two witty wives form an alliance which, while ostensibly aimed at shaming a philandering knight with designs on their chastity, is also targeted at the horn-mad husband of one of them, Mistress Ford.[28]

As in the case of Mercutio and Romeo and Benedict and his companions, jesting creates a bond between the two women, united against the shameless predations and paranoia of the opposite sex. What incenses them most is the thought that their pleasure in laughter is used as a weapon against them. In the (identical) love letter addressed to both women, Falstaff spells out why he assumes they will be willing to dally with him. 'You are not young; no more am I. Go to, then, there's sympathy. You are merry; so am I. Ha, ha, then there's more sympathy. You love sack, and so do I. Would you desire better sympathy?' (2.1.5–8). Ludicrous as this list is as seductive bait, it gestures towards a more serious issue: the widespread assumption that women's indulgence in mirth was evidence of their immorality. Mistress Page is infuriated that her merriment during their encounters, however restrained, has been deciphered as susceptibility to sexual temptation and availability for any aging roué to fulfil his lust. 'I'll exhibit a bill in the parliament for the putting down of men!' (24–25), she fumes, before resolving to take revenge. The impetus that fuels the two women's punitive plans is pithily summed up by Mistress Page later in the play: 'We'll leave a proof by that which we will do,/Wives may be merry and yet honest too' (4.2.92–3). Women, they insist, can enjoy jesting without jeopardising their honour, which, for women, meant one thing: chastity.[29] Their jesting is intended to embellish their reputation as patterns of virtue in order to carve out a space for themselves in which they will be able to give free rein to their desire for gaiety.

The importance of a woman's reputation is attested to by the large number of defamation cases brought by women during the early modern period. Most of these cases concerned sexual morality; an increasing number of them were brought by women against other women.[30] Sexual insults played a role for men, too, but men also sued their neighbours for libellous allegations about their general morals, their probity, or their religious conduct. Women's reputations stood and fell with their putative sexual behaviour. Any whiff of slander would have a devastating impact on their character and would additionally have implications for the social standing of their husband and family. Historians such as Susan Dwyer Amussen read these patterns of litigation as a corollary of the increasingly restricted role allotted to women in early modern society. Significantly, Mistress Page's first response to Falstaff's letter is to scrutinise her own behaviour. Even while railing on Falstaff as a drunkard, she wonders: 'What an unweighed behaviour hath this Flemish drunkard picked, with the devil's name, out of my conversation, that he dares in this manner assay me?' (19–21). Shakespeare explores the ramifications of sexual slurs on women in a number of plays, most notably in his tragedy about sexual jealousy, *Othello*. But horn-mad lovers or husbands also play a role in *Much Ado About Nothing*, *Cymbeline*, and *The Winter's Tale*, all plays in which plot entanglements involving suspicious men steer the comedies or romances close to tragedy.

Master Ford shares Falstaff's view of the dubious morals of women. When Ford and Page are approached by the resentful retainers of Falstaff, Pistol, and Nym, keen to disseminate malicious gossip about the employer who has just sacked them, the diverging responses of the two husbands speak volumes about their personality. In characteristically bombastic style, Pistol warns Master Ford that the knight is plotting to seduce his wife, ending on a dramatic note: 'Oh, odious is the name!' When the mystified Ford demands clarity, Pistol elaborates: 'The horn', adding helpfully, 'Take heed, ere summer comes, or cuckoo/Birds do sing' (2.1.109; 114–115). Cuckoos, known for letting other birds hatch their own eggs, were proverbially associated with cuckoldry. Ford immediately resolves to investigate the matter, confiding to the audience: ''Twas a sensible fellow' (131). His gullibility to the bluster of a braggart like Pistol, with whom spectators would have been familiar from the recently staged *Henry IV Part 2*, marks

Ford out as a comic butt from the very start. Page, on the other hand, accosted by the equally asinine Nim, promptly dismisses him, commenting in an aside, 'I never heard such a drawling, affecting rogue' (127). And while Page clearly trusts his wife and declares that if what they have heard about Falstaff's intentions is true, he would actively encourage his wife to meet the fat libertine, in full confidence in her ability to cut him down to size, Ford sees things quite differently. Although he admits he has no reason to doubt his wife, he mutters ominously, 'A man may be too confident' (167). In a few deft lines, Shakespeare offers a glimpse into the mind of a man whose mistrust of his wife masks an almost obscene eagerness to be cuckolded.

Ford initiates a plot to trap Mistress Ford, virtually bribing the debauched knight to seduce his wife. The evidence for her susceptibility to temptation that he puts forward is the well-worn notion that a fun-loving woman is inevitably licentious. Assuming the character of another suitor, one Master Broom, Ford confides in Falstaff, 'Some say that, though she appear honest to me, yet in other places she enlargeth her mirth so far that there is shrewd construction made of her' (2.2.197–200). At Falstaff's bemusement at the supposed competitor giving him precedence, 'Master Broom' explains that the knight will prepare the way for his own conquest of Mistress Ford. Once she has succumbed to one lover, she will be fair game for all the others. For once, the rascally knight is lost for words.

When he is alone, Ford gives vent to his true thoughts. His words, however comical, uncannily foreshadow those uttered by Othello in a play written only a few years later. Ford misconstrues what he hears about the appointment his wife has granted Falstaff and assumes that her adultery is a foregone conclusion: 'See the hell of having a false woman!', he rages. On even flimsier evidence, Othello leaps to similar conclusions about Desdemona's faithlessness. 'I had rather be a toad/ And live upon the vapor of a dungeon/Than keep a corner in the thing I love/For others' uses' (Oth. 3.3.268–271), Othello avows. 'I will rather trust a Fleming with my butter, Parson Hugh the Welshman with my cheese, an Irishman with my aqua-vitae bottle, or a thief to walk my ambling gelding, than my wife with herself', Ford fulminates, reeling off a string of jestbook clichés involving the addiction of Dutchmen to butter, Welshmen to cheese, Irishmen to whisky, and thieves to stealing horses, all of whom would be more trustworthy than his wife. And like Othello, whose eloquence during his epileptic fit dissolves into a cascade of fragments: 'Handkerchief! Confessions! Handkerchief!' (4.1.34–35), Ford's soliloquy culminates in a breakdown of language. 'Fie, fie, fie! Cuckold, cuckold, cuckold' (276–277), he splutters, in a moment that teeters between the farcical and the pathetic.

It is fully consistent with Ford's desire to exert dominance over his wife that he display jealousy about female friendship, which threatens to undermine his control. When he sees Mistress Page head for his home, he grouses, 'I think if your husbands were dead, you two would marry.' Mistress Page parries his attack with the words, 'Be sure of that—two other husbands' (3.2.11–13), smartly deflating his self-importance by hinting that he is entirely dispensable. Unleashing a series of jests or practical jokes against both the lecherous interloper and the horn-mad husband welds the two merry wives together in a coalition of shared interests. When they succeed in turning the tables on both men, Mistress Page crows, 'Is there not a double excellency in this?', while Mistress Ford confesses, 'I know not which pleases me better, that my husband is deceived, or Sir John' (3.3.148–150). For Mistress Page and Mistress Ford, jesting is a means to demonstrate their wit and boost their profile in the eyes of their husbands as well as the group of neighbours who populate the play. Their pranks foster the social cohesion of the world in which they live, reaffirming the values they share—companionship and decorum—while promoting those they themselves consider important, a free-spirited enjoyment of conviviality for women without compromising their reputation. Their jests, while directed at elements they consider a threat to these values, such as the sexually aggressive knight and the jealous spouse, do not necessarily culminate in ostracism of the deviant members of society. They are careful not to humiliate Master Ford to the extent that he loses face among his neighbours. And Falstaff too, once chastised, is welcomed back into the community. The play ends with Mistress Page reiterating her husband's invitation to the company, explicitly including the disgraced knight: 'let us everyone go home/And laugh this sport o'er by a country fire,/Sir John and all' (5.5.217–219).

JESTING AS A STRATEGY OF DEFENCE

A rich source of humour, theorists tell us, are the anxieties and preoccupations that define a given society. If at one level, jokes about cuckoldry reveal male fears of female assertiveness, jokes by women make capital out of female fears of being stifled, intimidated, or repressed in a patriarchal world. A country which has hurtled into the twenty-first century in the last few decades, India, has recently seen a variety of witty, feisty female stand-up comedians emerge within the fledgling comedy circuit aimed at the highly urban, English-speaking segments of Indian society.[31] Their comic material revolves around topics that are of visceral concern to women living in contemporary Indian society. Urooj Ashfaq, for instance, mines the insecurities of a young Muslim woman in a predominantly, and increasingly aggressive, Hindu environment, while Sejal Bhat recounts funny anecdotes about growing up in a conservative Indian household, spinning absurd tales about strict instructions to keep her underwear on at all times, including under the shower, and the way she and her sister plot to circumvent the rules. Most of the comics cater to an elite, Anglicised public in metropolitan centres like Mumbai or Delhi, and perform in English with a smattering of Hindi thrown in, the lingo of the urban elite in India today. There are notable exceptions, such as Deepika Mhatre, a former domestic help whose stand-up routine, performed in Hindi, consists of skewering the callous snobbery of her former employers—to an audience largely made up of the same class. A standard throwaway gag she utilises is relating how special she is; so special, in fact, that her employers have special tableware for her.[32] The satirical point is that the servant who prepares the food the family consume is considered too degraded to use the plates from which they consume it. The joke is a blistering send-up of elite circles, in which the lingering remnants of casteism blend seamlessly with modern class prejudice.

Many of the jokes by female comics tackle the taboos in women's lives in a society strait-jacketed in prudish norms. These strictures, the legacy of the colonial era, have received a powerful boost from the rise of Hindu fundamentalism on the subcontinent since the 1980s. Drawing on the staple comic theme of excrement, Radhika Vaz has fashioned a comic routine mocking women's corporal anxieties, for instance, in relation to defecation, while Aditi Mittal, a stalwart of Indian female comedy, has made a name for herself riffing on the theme of female shame, lampooning a world in which women need to take on supercilious male salesmen when buying a bra and girls are told by their male sports instructor to stay well away from him when they have their period (Figure 2.2). In her show, 'Things They Wouldn't Let me Say', she plays on the epithet of the Dark Lord in Harry Potter novels, 'He Who Must Not Be Named', quipping that 'saying the word "sanitary napkin" in public is like standing in a Hogwarts' common room and saying "Voldemort"'.[33] The budding comic landscape in India received a decisive impulse in 2013 from a satirical video produced by the All India Bakchod, a comedy collective known for its YouTube podcast and channel.[34] Titled 'It's Your Fault', the clip responded to the horrific gang rape of a young woman in Delhi in 2012. In the style of a commercial, a beautiful young woman smiles winningly into the camera and warbles, 'Ladies, did you think rape is something men do out of a desire for control, empowered by years of patriarchy?

Figure 2.2 *Aditi Mittal: Things They Wouldn't Let Me Say* (2017), Dir. Fazilla Alana, produced by Netflix Studios

You've clearly been misled by the notion that women are people too.' Without batting an eyelid, she proceeds to clear up the misconception to which so many women have succumbed. 'Rape: it's your fault', she explains patiently and lectures the spectators that it's women's manner of dress that provokes men to rape them. Meanwhile, the film displays a sequence of stills with provocative clothing that 'could cause rape'. These range from shorts, mini-skirts, long skirts, burqas, plastic overalls, to astronaut suits.[35] The film ends with a series of real-life women obediently chanting, 'It's my fault.' The clip, a savage caricature of the official response to the explosion in cases of violent rape in India, went viral. No doubt the smart Youtube comedians and the businesses that supported them espoused a feminist stance for their own purposes, catering to the Indian millennials who abhorred what they deemed was Neolithic behaviour. Nonetheless, the rage and frustration among Indian women that they capitalised on was very real.

Themes of female shame and the culture of surveillance to which women are subjected (and have internalised) remain of enduring interest, whether in contemporary society or in Shakespeare's time. As does humour as a female defence strategy. Both play a central role in *Much Ado About Nothing*, whose plot turns on the cruel jest played on Hero, tricking her into believing she is to be married only to expose her to the supreme humiliation of being shamed at the altar. Beatrice persistently mocks the male mania about cuckoldry that pervades the play. In Act 2 scene 1, she and her uncle Leonato, depicted in a joking relationship of easy camaraderie, bandy jests about marriage and infidelity back and forth. In what might be termed a double act, Leonato, here aided by his brother Antonio, takes on the role of straight man and feeds her comic cues.

Leonato:	By my troth, niece, thou wilt never get thee a husband if thou be so shrewd of thy tongue.
Anthony:	In faith, she's too curst.
Beatrice:	Too curst is more than curst. I shall lessen God's sending that way, for it is said, 'God sends a curst cow short horns, but to a cow too curst, he sends none.'
Leonato:	So, by being too curst, God will send you no horns?
Beatrice:	Just, if he send me no husband, for the which blessing I am at him upon my knees every morning and evening.

(2.1.16–25)

When the two old men lament the sharpness of Beatrice's tongue (she is too 'curst'), she seizes on the qualifier 'too' and turns it into a punning reference to two horns, citing the proverbial saying that since God spreads defects evenly among his creatures, a bad-tempered cow does not possess horns. In another imaginative leap, she draws a link between herself and the hornless cow in the adage, asserting that the only way to avoid being betrayed by a husband is be too sharp-tongued to ever to get married in the first place. Beatrice triumphantly turns the male discourse about cuckoldry (you can't trust a woman) on its head, declaring that in truth, you can never trust a man.

Beatrice spins out the joke about cuckoldry even further. Her ideal fate, she contends, would be to remain unmarried. She resorts to yet another proverb to paint a picture of an idyllic afterlife. She would happily lead apes into hell, she announces, a fate supposedly reserved for old maids. She elaborates a fantasy anecdote about meeting the devil, who, 'like an old cuckold with horns on his head', would direct her to heaven. There St Peter would show her 'where the bachelors sit, and there live we, as merry as the day is long' (37; 40–41), she concludes.[36]

Beatrice sends up the entire male obsession with cuckoldry as a huge joke. As she reminds us, horns can mean many things—the devil, for example, is often represented as horned. The ambivalence of horn symbolism is something Shakespeare himself plays with. In *The Merry Wives of Windsor*, Falstaff is proud of the antlers he dons as the (fictitious) Herne the Hunter, addressing the mythological king of gods, Jupiter, as a brother in arms: 'Jove, thou wast a bull for thy Europa. Love set on thy horns' (5.5.3). For Falstaff, horns are a sign of potency and align him with Jupiter in the guise of a bull. In *As You Like It*, the courtiers sing a hunting song wryly equating antlers with a cuckold's horns and exhorting other men to accept their fate with dignity: 'Take thou no scorn to wear the horn./ It was a crest e'er thou wast born./Thy father's father wore it./And thy father bore it' (4.2.14–17). And in his defence of marriage, Touchstone delivers a facetious defence of cuckoldry as an inevitable element in human life. 'As horns are odious, they are necessary', he argues. He too adduces deer as fellow horn-bearers and points out that, never mind horns, being married is preferable to being a bachelor. He concludes, 'by how much defence is better than no skill, by so much is horn more precious than to want' (3.3.43; 51–53), ending his jocular debate with himself with a pun on the image of the horn of plenty.

Unlike the jokes about cuckoldry cracked by Benedict, Beatrice's vision of paradise reveals a different set of ideals. While Benedict yearns for a world without women, where men would be companionable without the distraction of the female sex, Beatrice dreams of a world of unmarried men and women in which equality between the sexes would reign. What prevents her from pursuing marriage is not the thought of male company, but the fear of male domination. As she jests to her uncle, 'Adam's son are my brethren, and, truly, I hold it a sin to match in my kindred' (53–55). If men and women are siblings, marriage is a kind of incest, she wisecracks.

For all her sparkling wit, Beatrice's jesting hints at a sadness beneath the facade of her merriness. Don Pedro, complimenting her on the acuity of her repartee, remarks, 'For out o'question, you were born in a merry hour' (2.1.294–295). 'No, sure, my lord, my mother cried', Beatrice contradicts him. 'But then there was a star danced, and under that was I born' (296–297). Beatrice's sprightly humour is hard-won, not a gift conferred on her. For Beatrice, as for so many of the female comics described earlier, jesting is a self-protective device, a strategy to which she resorts to negotiate a restrictive world in which the equality between the sexes of which she dreams is at a premium. Leonato describes what Hero has observed about her cousin: 'she hath often dreamt of unhappiness and waked herself with laughing' (305–306). For Beatrice, humour is a tool of resilience in the face of a bleak reality.

ROSALIND AND ROMANTIC DEFLATION

Rosalind belongs to a slew of supremely confident female characters that people Shakespeare's drama. These include Cleopatra, the ladies in *Love's Labour's Lost*, Portia in *The Merchant of Venice*, Queen Margaret in *Henry VI Part 3*, Lady Macbeth, and Paulina in *The Winter's Tale*, to name only the most outstanding figures. What sets Rosalind apart is a unique blend of wit, pleasure in play, and ironic scepticism towards gender ideology. Beneath an exuberant exterior, however, Rosalind reflects the vulnerability of women in a society governed by a double standard, in which articulating desire would entail social vilification as depraved.

Shakespeare is fond of utilising the device of cross-dressing to explore gender norms. The ploy is given a self-reflexive comic twist from the fact that all female roles were played by boy actors. Among Shakespeare's numerous cross-dressed heroines, only in the case of Portia and Rosalind does pleasure in playacting take precedence over expediency. To be sure, female disguise is always linked to a plot twist that makes it imperative for the female protagonist to impersonate a man. For Portia, adopting the role of a lawyer requires a male disguise, while for Rosalind donning male attire is a means to facilitate the escape of herself and Celia from the court of Duke Frederick. And yet, Rosalind's delight at the thought of changing into a swaggering youth is palpable. As she says to Celia (who merely dresses up as a maid), 'in my heart—/Lie there what hidden woman's fear there will—/We'll have a swashing and martial outside/As many other mannish cowards have' (1.3.114–117). Rosalind immediately grasps the fact that masculinity is a matter of performance. In the same way as men adopt a stance of self-assertive manliness to evoke the impression of virile qualities that they may not possess, masquerading as a bold young man will help mask her fear—and perhaps even enable her to reinvent herself and acquire the confidence she hankers after. Her disguise achieves the desired goal: she metamorphoses into one of Shakespeare's surrogate dramatists, a select band that includes characters like Oberon, Vincentio, Paulina, and Prospero, and takes firm charge of the rest of the play.

Under cover of being a youth, significantly named Ganymede, Rosalind, played by a boy, embarks on an extended

game of jesting flirtation with Orlando in which sexual bina-
ries swirl around in a breathtaking vortex of mutual erotic
attraction.[37] Rosalind too cracks a cuckoldry joke, comparing
men to snails: what both share are horns. The difference is
that the snail 'brings his destiny with him' (4.1.50) instead of
dallying until horns are imposed on him. But the message that
Rosalind wants to impart to Orlando is not that women are
invariably unfaithful. Instead, in the guise of an androgynous
young man who moves effortlessly between sexual boundaries, she attempts to tell him what human relations are like
in reality, as opposed to the idealised Petrarchan sphere that
Orlando inhabits. After playing at getting betrothed, Orlando
solemnly vows he will love her (or him) forever. Rosalind
refuses to accept his effusive declaration of passion. Rejecting
the lyrical medium of verse, she insists on using robust prose.
Once she is married, she declares, 'I will be more jealous of
thee than a Barbary cock-pigeon over his hen, more clamorous than a parrot against rain, more newfangled than an
ape, more giddy in my desires than a monkey' (130–133). In
addition, she asserts, she will weep when he is feeling cheerful, and laugh 'like a hyena' (135) when he is drowsy. Using
wit as a tool, Rosalind sets out to demolish Orlando's mawk-
ish ideas of love.

Rosalind has other goals in her sights as well. By purport-
ing to reveal to Orlando what the woman he loves will be
like in everyday life, she mockingly dismantles the opposition
between angelic women and debased specimens of woman-
hood that for centuries has shaped male attitudes towards
women. Above all, Rosalind emphatically warns Orlando
against any attempt to muzzle women's wit, embracing all
the varied connotations of the term. Any bid to rein in wom-
en's minds, their imagination, and their verbal dexterity is

doomed to fail: 'Make the doors upon a woman's wit and it will out at the casement; shut that and 'twill out at the key-hole; stop that, 'twill fly with the smoke out at the chimney' (141–144), she avers.

Rosalinds' own ability to range within the zodiac of her wit is demonstrated at its most brilliant in her debunking of classical myths of love. When Orlando makes yet another cloying avowal of love, insisting he will die if he cannot possess her, she retorts,

> The poor world is almost six thousand years old, and in all this time there was not any man died in his own person, *videlicet* in a love cause. Troilus had his brains dashed out with a Grecian club; yet he did what he could to die before, and he is one of the patterns of love. Leander, he would have lived many a fair year though Hero had turned nun, if it had not been for a hot midsummer night; for, good youth, he went but forth to wash him in the Hellespont, and, being taken with the cramp, was drowned, and the foolish chroniclers of that age found it was Hero of Sestos. But these are all lies: men have died from time to time, and worms have eaten them, but not for love.

(4.1.82–94)

In a set piece of undiluted bathos, Rosalind sabotages the hackneyed fantasies of romantic love that her culture, like ours, is steeped in, and that serve to gloss over gender inequalities and double standards. Men have never died of a broken heart, she maintains. Classical exemplars of love such as Troilus or Leander died in battle or of cramps, but not of love. Rosalind's caustic wit exposes the game of wooing as a charade. In a flash of ironic self-awareness, Rosalind's humour also reflects back on herself. Deeply infatuated with Orlando, she is not immune to amorous clichés, as her response betrays when she first hears of her lover's presence in the forest: 'he comes to kill my heart!' (3.2.227). Her words evoke a brief moment of distance from herself in which she knows that the joke is on her, too.

Rosalind's devaluation of the classical tradition also takes a sideswipe at a field of learning that was debarred to most women. The deflation of prestigious, male-dominated arenas of cultural knowledge is still a fertile source of humour for contemporary female comedians. Hannah Gadsby, for instance, takes a look at famous artworks that portray the ancient world, such as Raphael's fresco, *The School of Athens*, a paean to the Greek philosophers whose ideas have defined Western thought. Among the throng of male philosophers, there is only one woman, Hypatia of Alexandria. What were all the women doing while the men were busy thinking, Hannah Gadsby wonders. She promptly delivers the answer. Displaying a series of paintings by artists such as Raphael and Rubens featuring the Three Graces, she concludes, 'Dancing naked in groups of three in the forest is the number one hobby of women at all times.' Moving on to paintings depicting the classical myth of Andromeda, waiting to be rescued by the Greek hero Perseus, she notes, 'Women getting stuck to rocks is the number two hobby of ladies at all times.'[38] Shakespeare's array of witty women and their precursors, the women in jestbook literature, still provide us with paradigms as to how women might harness the power of humour for their varied concerns.

NOTES

1 Cited in *Oxford Dictionary of Humorous Quotations*, ed. Ned Sherrin, 2nd ed., Oxford Paperback Reference (Oxford: Oxford University Press, 2004), 155.

2 For an overview of research, see Helga Kotthoff, 'Gender and Humor: The State of the Art', *Journal of Pragmatics* 38.1 (2006), 4–25. On gendered discourse see Penelope Eckert and Sally McConnell-Ginet, *Language and Gender*, 2nd ed. (Cambridge: Cambridge University Press, 2013). A foundational study is Deborah Tannen, *Gender and Discourse* (Oxford: Oxford University Press, 1994).

3 Giselinde Kuipers, *Good Humor, Bad Taste: A Sociology of the Joke* (Berlin: De Gruyter, 2015).

4 Judith Butler, *Gender Trouble: Feminism and the Subversion of Identity* (New York: Routledge, 1990) is the classic articulation of a performative theory of gender.

5 Robert R. Provine, *Laughter: A Scientific Investigation* (London: Faber and Faber, 2000), especially 23–53.

6 Since the 1960s, a wave of feminist cultural criticism has dissected this development. More specifically, critics have identified a sharp distinction between women considered virtuous (mothers, wives, sisters) and those considered to be successors of Eve, deceitful and seductive. One important study is Judith R. Walkowitz, *City of Dreadful Delight: Narrative of Sexual Danger in Late-Victorian London* (Chicago: University of Chicago Press, 1992).

7 See Anthony Fletcher, *Gender, Sex and Subordination in England 1500–1800* (New Haven, CT: Yale University Press, 1995) for an overview of the change in gender relations.

8 'The female is as it were a deformed male.' See Aristotle, *Generation of Animals*, trans. A. L. Peck, Loeb Classical Library (Cambridge, MA: Harvard University Press, 1942), 737a.

9 *Upstart Crow*, Season 1, Episode 6.

10 See the path-breaking essay by Nancy F. Cott, 'Passionlessness: An Interpretation of Victorian Sexual Ideology, 1790–1850', *Signs* 4.2 (Winter, 1978): 219–36.

11 See Daniel Wickberg, *The Senses of Humor: Self and Laughter in Modern America* (Ithaca, NY: Cornell University Press, 1998) and Stuart M. Tave, *The Amiable Humorist: A Study in the Comic Theory and Criticism of the Eighteenth and Early Nineteenth Centuries* (Chicago: University of Chicago Press, 1960).

12 *Michelle Wolf: Joke Show* (Netflix Comedy Special, 2019).

13 See Karen Newman, *Fashioning Femininity and English Renaissance Drama* (Chicago: University of Chicago Press, 1993), 3–12. Also see Suzanne E. Hull,

Chaste, Silent and Obedient: English Books for Women, 1475–1640 (San Marino: Huntington Library, 1982).

14 Juan Luis Vives, *A very fruitfull and pleasante booke, called the Instruction of a Christian woman*, trans. Richard Hyrde (1585), J5v.

15 Ibid., J2r-v.

16 Ibid., S3v-4r.

17 Richard Brathwaite, *The English Gentleman and English Gentlewoman* (1641), 2T1v; 2Q2v.

18 See Phil Withington, '"Tumbled into the Dirt": Wit and Incivility in Early Modern England', in *Understanding Historical (Im)politeness: Relational Linguistic Practice Over Time and across Cultures*, ed. Marcel Bax and Daniel Z. Kadar (Amsterdam: John Benjamins, 2012), 154–74.

19 The deflation of heroism in the play is wittily explored in Emma Smith, *This is Shakespeare* (London: Pelican Books, 2019), 255–70.

20 'The Life of Marcus Antonius', *Plutarch's Lives of Noble Grecians and Romanes*, trans. Sir Thomas North (1579), in *Narrative and Dramatic Sources of Shakespeare*, ed. Geoffrey Bullough, Vol. 5 (London: Routledge and Kegan Paul, 1964), 275.

21 Ibid. A 'slent' is 'a sly hit or sarcasm', while in this passage 'finely' could refer to 'in a subtle manner'. See 'slent, n.1' 3 and 'finely, adv. and adj.' 3, *Oxford English Dictionary Online*.

22 For two important studies on unruly women and the battle of the sexes, respectively, see Zemon Davis, *Society and Culture in Early Modern France*, esp. 124–51, and Linda Woodbridge, *Women and the English Renaissance: Literature and the Nature of Womankind, 1540–1620* (Urbana, IL: University of Illinois Press, 1984).

23 Tim Reinke-Williams, 'Misogyny, Jest-Books and Male Youth Culture in Seventeenth-Century England', *Gender and History* 21.2 (2009): 324–39.

24 For an account of women's appropriation of jest literature for their own purposes, see Pamela Allen Brown, *Better a Shrew than a Sheep: Women, Drama and the Culture of Jest in Early Modern England* (Ithaca, NY: Cornell University Press, 2003).

25 Rastell, *A Hundred Merry Tales: The Shakespeare Jest Book*, 210.

26 Cicero, *Brutus, Orator*, trans. G. L. Hendrickson and H. M. Hubbell, Loeb Classical Library (Cambridge, MA: Harvard University Press, 1939), 75–90.

27 John Taylor, *Wit and Mirth*, in *All the workes of John Taylor the water-poet* (1630), 2S1r-v.

28 A useful collection of critical essays on the play is *The Merry Wives of Windsor: New Critical Essays*, ed. Evelyn Gajowski and Phyllis Rackin (Routledge, 2015). Also see the discussion in Brown, *Better a Shrew than a Sheep*, 43–55.

29 At the time the term 'honest' still retained a close link to the notion of honour, from which it derived, and only gradually gained the meaning of truthfulness. See 'honest, adj.', *Oxford English Dictionary Online*.

30 Susan Dwyer Amussen, *An Ordered Society: Gender and Class in Early Modern England* (New York: Columbia University Press, 1988), 98–104.

31 See www.lifestyleasia.com/ind/culture/entertainment/best-female-stand-up-comedians-in-india/, accessed August 2020.

32 https://indianexpress.com/article/trending/trending-in-india/maid-turned-comedian-story-5297929/, accessed August 2020.

33 *Aditi Mittal: Things They Wouldn't Let Me Say* (Netflix Comedy Special, 2017).

34 The title is a parody of the national state-run broadcaster, All India Radio; the term 'bakhchod' is urban Hindi slang for 'bullshitter'. The company, subsequently mired in scandal, closed down in 2019.

35 www.youtube.com/watch?v=8hC0Ng_ajpY

36 The term 'bachelor' refers to both unmarried men and women.

37 On the fluidity of sexual desire in the play, see especially Valerie Traub, 'The Homoerotics of Shakespearean Comedy', in *Desire and Anxiety: Circulations of Sexuality in Shakespearean Drama* (London: Routledge, 1992), 117–44.

38 *Hannah Gadsby: Douglas* (Nexflix Comedy Special, 2020).

'Wise enough to play the fool'

Twelfth Night 3.1.53

The speaker of T. S. Eliot's dramatic monologue, 'The Love Song of J. Alfred Prufrock', wonders whether he is a modern Hamlet, only to discard the idea: 'No! I am not Prince Hamlet, nor was meant to be.'[1] As he does throughout the poem, Prufrock misses the point. The epitome of mediocrity and pusillanimity, he is certainly not a tragic hero. What he does share with the Prince is a preoccupation with overwhelming questions, a profound sense of loneliness, and endless self-absorption. And like Shakespeare's tragedy, the poem captures the spirit of uncertainty that permeates modernity. Prufrock finally admits that he 'almost ridiculous/Almost, at times, the Fool'.[2] But Prufrock is not a Shakespearean fool. Shakespeare's fools at court or in noble households are not figures of ridicule. They are supremely self-assured professionals, virtuosi in the art of verbal legerdemain and mocking innuendo. *Hamlet* itself is a play without a professional fool (except for a dead jester, Yorick, whose skull has become iconic for the play). It does, however, offer a number of surrogates. They include the grave-digger, who bests Hamlet at chop-logic—and the Prince himself, whose caustic wit provides much of the humour of the play.

DOI: 10.4324/9780429317507-4

There are marked affinities between Shakespeare's clowns and fools and professional comedians in today's entertainment industry. This might be because as in-house playwright and sharer in one of the most successful theatre companies of the time, the Lord Chamberlain's Men, Shakespeare created his plays with bespoke roles for the star comedians in the company. Critics such as David Wiles and Bart van Es have meticulously traced the way his work was a creative partnership based on close collaboration with the actors, in particular with two outstanding comic performers, William Kemp and Robert Armin.[3] The styles of both comedians were very different and have shaped the variety of clowns and fools in Shakespeare's comedies.

SHAKESPEARE'S CLOWNS

The doyen of Elizabethan stage comedians was Richard Tarlton. Immortalised in numerous allusions in plays (Yorick might have been a tribute to him too) and in jests that circulated decades after his death in 1588, some of them in a jest-book named after him, *Tarltons Jests* (1613), he was one of the first stage celebrities.[4] His comic circuit encompassed performances on stage in London and provincial towns, at court and in the tavern. He was the first Elizabethan comedian to achieve stardom on a national scale.[5] Although born and bred in London, his stock persona was that of a rustic in the city, a mixture of the innocent abroad and the wily country bumpkin. His hallmark seems to have been a knack for extemporising and engaging directly with the audience in crosstalk. Andrew Gurr attributes the shift in meaning of the word 'clown' from 'peasant' to 'comedian', which took place in this period and that can be traced in early modern playscripts, largely to Tarlton's influence. In Shakespeare's plays, both meanings are often conflated with each other—the country bumpkin *was* the funny man.[6]

Tarlton's fame cast a long shadow, and all future comedians would grapple with his legacy, either by emulating him or by defining themselves against his brand of humour. William Kemp, leading comedian in the Lord Chamberlain's Men until his departure in 1599, adopted Tarlton's persona of a plain-speaking commoner and was apparently equally adroit in extemporising, but his roles were far more closely integrated into the plot of the play. A talented dancer, his main strength lay in performing jigs, the rambunctious song-and-dance playlets that ended a theatre performance.[7] They were hugely popular, and might have catered additionally to spectators who could not afford theatre tickets and flocked to the theatre after the plays ended. After Kemp left, Shakespeare's company dropped jigs altogether, although they remained in the repertoires of more downmarket playhouses in the north of London. Why Kemp parted company with his fellow actor-sharers remains unclear, but perhaps Hamlet's admonition to the players contains a clue. It hints at friction between the comedian who regarded a play as a star vehicle and the priorities of the rest of the company: 'let those that play your clowns speak no more than is set down for them; for there be of them that will themselves laugh to set on some quantity of barren spectators to laugh too, though in the meantime some necessary question of the play be then to be considered. That's villainous, and shows a most pitiful ambition in the fool that uses it' (*Hamlet* 3.2.34–40). Hamlet as self-appointed impresario is scathing about clowns who spin out a comic routine to bask in audience laughter at the expense of the rest of the players, who need to carry on with the business of the play.

The comic roles Shakespeare created while Kemp was the chief clown of the company are quite different from the later roles for wise fools, tailored to Robert Armin, Kemp's replacement as comic lead. They span a range of low-status characters, including Lance, Costard, Bottom, Lancelet Gobbo, and Dogberry, on whom Shakespeare tries out an array of comic devices. In *The Two Gentlemen of Verona*, two comical servants, close cousins of the witty slaves in Roman New Comedy, provide a foretaste of comedic patterns that Shakespeare will repeat throughout his work. The early jokes are time-honoured samples of comic patter. The whip-smart Speed outwits one of the Veronese gentlemen, Proteus, in repartee, compelling him to admit, 'Beshrew me but you have a quick wit.' 'And yet it cannot overtake your slow purse', Speed fires back, triggering the monetary reward he desires (1.1.119–20). His less quick-witted colleague, Lance, is furnished with a farcical and unfailingly hilarious routine about his hard-hearted dog Crab, who refuses to shed a tear at their family farewell. A trademark of Shakespeare's doltish clowns is their propensity for malapropism, particularly when they are trying hard to ape their betters. Lance announces, 'I have received my proportion, like the prodigious son, and am going with Sir Proteus to the Imperial's court' (2.3.2–4), managing to mangle two words in one sentence. He replaces 'Emperor' with its adjective, and more drolly, the term 'prodigal son' with the words 'prodigious son', which at the time meant freakish or strange. Lance also indulges in some comic business with props, taking off his shoes to create a tableau of the tearful parting from his family. He promptly gets confused. 'This shoe is my father. No, this left shoe is my father. No, no, this left shoe is my mother. Nay, that cannot be so neither. Yes, it is so, it is so: it hath the worser sole', he declares, his egregious pun on 'sole' a sly jibe at the arcane medieval debate whether women had souls. For good measure, he throws in a ribald jest: 'This shoe with the hole in it is my mother, and this my father' (13–6).

The joke lies in Lance's ludicrous relationship to both animals and objects, both of which he treats as if they were human, but the play also contains jokes which convey a subtle comment on the themes of the play.[8] Once again, Lance's bad-tempered dog Crab has a star turn. Lance has followed his master to the grand household of the Duke of Milan and observes Crab's botched attempts at canine social climbing: 'He thrusts me himself into the company of three or four gentleman-like dogs under the Duke's table. He had not been there—bless the mark—a pissing while but all the chamber smelt him. "Out with the dog," says one; "What cur is that?" says another; "Whip him out," says the third; "Hang him up," says the Duke' (4.4.14–19). To save his pet from a whipping, Lance takes the blame for the pissing debacle. Who else would sacrifice himself for his dog, he ponders, and turning to Crab, tells him sternly, 'Thou think'st not of this now' (30).

In a play concerned with notions of civility and the pursuit of cultural capital, the anecdote of Crab's disastrous failure at upward mobility is a joke whose target is not only the characters of the play, but the aspirations of the audience, similarly preoccupied with questions of status. At the same time, Lance's unflinching loyalty to his companion, however absurd the lengths to which he is prepared to go for him, sheds an unflattering light on the alacrity with which the gentlemen of the play betray each other and the women they claim to love.

Increasingly, Shakespeare would use clownish characters to enrich the argument of the play. In *Love's Labour's Lost*, the rustic Costard is only one of a line-up of buffoons that the play presents, albeit the lowest-ranking of them. The clique of noblemen around whom the plot is woven is determined to set up an academy of learning in Navarre. Clowns like Costard are by definition outside the bounds of the magic circle. Apart from the pratfalls of the preening aristocrats, part of the humour of the play derives from Costard's deflationary plain speech. In florid terms, the vainglorious Spanish knight Armado accuses him of breaking the edict of chastity and consorting with 'a child of our grandmother Eve' or 'the weaker vessel'. Costard, once he grasps what Armado is blathering about, is happy to 'confess the wench' (1.1.250; 257; 265).

But like the rest of the Navarrese, Costard too succumbs to the allure of high-flown language, particularly when coupled with material gain. When receiving payment, portentously termed 'remuneration' by Armado, Costard is delighted with the shiny new word. '"Remuneration"? Oh, that's the Latin word for three farthings. Three farthings: remuneration. "What's the price of this inkle?" "One penny." "No, I'll give you a remuneration." . . . Why, it is a fairer name than "French crown." I will never buy and sell out of this word' (3.1.126–31).

The passage piles up a profusion of jokes in a few lines. Doing the yokel in different voices, Costard acts out a playlet in which he is both buyer and seller of a mundane item, linen tape (or 'inkle'), the banality of which contrasts with the pomposity of the word he so lovingly repeats. His understanding of the term is just sufficiently off-kilter to be funny: he thinks it means a specific sum of money, to be precise, the amount that he has received from Armado. He makes a patriotic stance in defence of the term (clearly ignorant of its French origin) in opposition to the expression 'French crown', which he seems to assume is another monetary term, instead of a reference to syphilis. Early modern spectators, weaned on a stream of jokes about the so-called 'French disease' (the English are fond of outsourcing their diseases), would no doubt have enjoyed the howlers of a low-life character to whom everyone could feel superior. In truth, however, Costard is an artful example of jokes that cut several ways—and include a jab at the audience. An embodiment of boorishness, he nonetheless serves to parody the elite characters of the play, who display the very same fascination with elevated language. As do the representatives of the educated classes, the pedant and the curate, who vie with each other in heaping up ever more bizarre turns of phrase. As Armado's page, the precocious Moth, remarks drily, 'They have been at a great feast of languages and stolen the scraps' (5.1.35–36). They all expect a reward for the rhetorical elegance they are so anxious to cultivate, be it in the form of enhanced social status or in cutting an impressive figure in the eyes of the sophisticated Ladies of France. And they all, in various ways, end up making fools of themselves, to a far greater extent than the clown. For those in the audience paying careful attention, this might cut close to the bone.

Of all Shakespeare's comedies, *Love's Labour's Lost*, with its carefully patterned verse and fireworks of wit, is the play that is most preoccupied with stylish language.[9] Its glittering idiom caters to an audience which for its part was in love with verbal play. But at the same time, the play dissects the vogue for language games that was such a feature of the Renaissance. It probes the dazzling facade of wit and reveals the crassness and self-regard at the heart of its characters, most glaringly in the Navarrese elite, who display a blithe disregard for keeping promises, breaking the oaths they themselves have devised. The most blistering comment on their ethical ambiguity is delivered by the illiterate clown, Costard. When asked by the King to leave the company of the aristocrats, he remarks mockingly, 'Walk aside, the true folk, and let the traitors stay' (4.3.207).

Shakespeare's clowns are frequently the fulcrum of a multi-layered joke. On one level, they are the butt of jokes about their obtuseness and foolishly inflated sense of importance. On another, they provide a distorted reflection of the characters of the main plot, inevitably of elite status, parodying their vanities and obsessions. In addition, they glance mockingly at traits many of us share with the protagonists of the plays. At rare moments, some of the most trenchant insights of the play are delivered by the clowns. For all their oafishness, the clowns are, almost, at times, truth-tellers.

SHAKESPEAREAN CLOWNS REDUX

The strategy of using simpletons to expose the idiocy of the rest of humanity is not one Shakespeare invented. Satire has flourished in every culture, as have clowns and jesters.[10] But given the enormous cultural resonance of Shakespeare's plays, his use of this comic device has decisively shaped later satire. Often the motif of the naive traveller replaces the Shakespearean figure of the rustic or lower-status buffoon in the great house. In *Gulliver's Travels*, Jonathan Swift takes aim both at eighteenth-century society and at the narrator himself, whose name betrays his main characteristic: an inexhaustible store of gullibility. A towering proponent of the Age of Enlightenment, Swift was unrelenting in his critique of many of its features, above all the optimistic view of human nature propagated by deist philosophers like Shaftesbury and Hutcheson. By presenting the travelogue from the viewpoint of a narrator noteworthy only for his ordinariness and his remarkable immunity to acquiring even a modicum of self-knowledge,

Swift subverts complacent enlightened beliefs in the educative value of human experience.

It is not that Gulliver learns nothing at all from his travels. Swift teases the reader with suggestions that by becoming aware of other ways of living, his narrator has garnered a smattering of insight. When he first finds himself in Brobdingnag, a land populated by giants, he is filled with horror at the monstrosity of the creatures. However, with time, he begins to see the world from their perspective:

> after having been accustomed several Months to the Sight and Converse of this People, and observed every Object upon which I cast my Eyes, to be of proportionable Magnitude; the Horror I had first conceived from their Bulk and Aspect was so far worn off, that if I had then beheld a Company of *English* Lords and Ladies in their Finery . . . Strutting and Bowing and Prating; to say the Truth, I should have been strongly tempted to laugh as much at them as the King and his Grandees did at me.[11]

It seems that Gulliver's frame of reference has shifted, and he realises how laughable his own countrymen appear to outsiders. But the illusion that Gulliver has changed soon evaporates. When he is dropped into the ocean by a giant bird and saved by a passing ship, he regards his saviours with disdain. Human beings appear to him as freaks of nature: 'I thought they were the most little contemptible Creatures I had ever beheld.' When he is finally reunited with his family, Gulliver thinks of them 'as if they had been Pigmies, and I a Giant' (137). Like New Age tourists to India who return laden with spiritual paraphernalia, Gulliver assimilates merely the superficial aspects of other cultures. Absurdly, he identifies himself with the gigantic size of the Brobdingnagians but imbibes not a shred of their enlightened political and social views.

This is most blatant at the end of his travels, when Gulliver returns from the land of the Houyhnhnms, a race of enlightened horses. Filled with hatred for his own kind, he yearns for a return to an island described in terms that evoke Plato's ideal Republic. He has adopted the art of neighing and trotting, and spends most of his time in his stable, shunning human contact to the extent possible. Nonetheless, he is determined 'to apply those excellent Lessons of Virtue which I learned among the Houyhnhnms; to instruct the Yahoos of my own Family as far as I shall find them docible Animals'. He begins his regimen of instruction with his wife, whom he permits to join him for dinner, although he insists that she sit at the farthest end of the table in order to escape her offensive smell. He is less forbearing towards other humans. In particular, he refuses to tolerate the vice of pride: 'when I behold a Lump of Deformity, and Diseases both in Body and Mind, smitten with Pride, it immediately breaks all the Measures of my Patience' (276). By making his grotesquely self-opinionated protagonist the object of ridicule, Swift simultaneously excoriates the hubris and self-righteousness of his contemporaries, who, at the time he was writing the book, were engaged on a sweeping quest to discover and colonise the rest of the world. Despite their continual close encounters with other cultures, Swift insinuates, his fellow countrymen have grasped precisely nothing about them, let alone broadened their stultified minds.

Gulliver sets off on his travels as a cheerful optimist and returns a misanthrope. Not all clownish characters undergo the same trajectory. The jejune traveller device has recently been adopted to satirical effect by the comedian Sacha Baron

Cohen, creator of the fictive Kazakhstani journalist Borat who journeys to the United States. The mockumentary *Borat: Cultural Learning of America for Make Benefit Glorious Nation of Kazakhstan* (2006), a spectacular success worldwide, was followed by a sequel in 2020, *Borat Subsequent Moviefilm*.[12] If in the first film the protagonist is on an assignment to investigate American mores, the premise of the sequel is slightly different. In disgrace for having harmed the reputation of Kazakhstan, Borat is only released by the ruler of the country on condition that he deliver a bribe to Mike Pence, Vice President of the United States at the time. When the chosen sweetener, consisting of Johnny the Monkey, who doubles as the Kazakh Minister of Culture, does not survive the trip, Borat seeks and gains permission to give his fifteen-year-old daughter Tutar as a sexual gift to Pence. In one of the provocative prank scenes for which Baron Cohen's comedy has become famous, Borat bursts into an American Conservative Union conference to offer Tutar to Pence, before being removed by security guards. Borat then decides to present Rudolph Giuliani, personal lawyer to President Donald Trump, with his teenage daughter. In the meantime, Tutar escapes from her father and embarks on a career as journalist herself. The hoax interview of Giuliani by the actress Maria Bakalova, who plays Tutar, where the seventy-six-year-old former Mayor of New York is caught on camera leering at the young reporter and generally behaving in an inappropriate manner, is the most sensational stunt of the film.

At first sight, the admittedly often crude gags of the film seem to be built around that perennial source of humour, the stupid foreigner, the contemporary equivalent of the country cousin. The bumbling Kazakh is lampooned for his backward views in everything ranging from anti-Semitism to attitudes about women. At a second glance, the joke redounds on the ostensibly more civilised nation the Eastern European duo are visiting. The dialogue bristles with outrageous racist statements and stereotypes, all of which are accepted with equanimity by the American citizens Borat encounters. In a hardware shop, he demands a bottle of propane gas and asks the salesman, 'How many gypsies could I finish with one cannister?' Without batting an eyelid, the latter advises him to 'take the bigger one'. In a bakery, the disguised comedian orders a cake with an anti-Semitic message in icing. Once again, the bakery employee obliges without the slightest objection. (The joke gestures ironically towards the *cause célèbre* of a baker in Colorado who in 2012 refused to create a wedding cake for a gay couple, citing religious scruples.)[13] Whether the people he meets accept the invidious sentiments expressed by Borat as typical of benighted foreigners, or whether they actively endorse them, they seem to find no reason not to play along as long as money changes hands. Perhaps more revealingly, the attitude that Borat evinces towards his daughter, whom he initially considers as a second-class specimen of humanity, whose only purpose can lie in securing favours of the powerful, is uncomfortably close to the views on offer in the glimpses of American culture provided by the film, in which, for instance, a clinic for plastic surgery never questions the decision of a father to have his teenage daughter submit to an operation to enhance her attractivity for potential spouses. In one hoax scene, the real-life Instagram influencer Macy Chanel is hired by Borat to teach his daughter how to become a 'sugar babe' to entice rich old men. Chanel's advice is to cultivate a feminine air of weakness. This, she claims, is what men like. The gap between a barbaric culture in which women are kept in cages, and one in which they are groomed to snare the prize of a wealthy husband, dwindles into insignificance.

Ironically, Chanel, whose work includes appearances on a dating site for 'sugar daddies', and who claims in an interview to have suspected that she was victim of a fraud during the filming of the scene, was nonetheless quick to capitalise on her role in the film by promoting it on her Instagram site, no doubt as an advertisement for her services.[14] At times reality outstrips satire.

The extent to which the audience of the film—or, for that matter, of a Shakespeare play—realise that the joke is on them is a moot point. Swift himself was less than optimistic about the effect of satire. As he notes, satire is 'a sort of glass wherein Beholders do generally discover every body's Face but their own; which is the chief Reason for that kind of Reception it meets with in the world, and that so very few are offended with it'.[15] Satire, we firmly believe, is always about other people.

THE WISE FOOL

Dogberry might have been the last clown to have been played by celebrity comedian Will Kemp.[16] When the Lord Chamberlain's Men relocated from East London to Southwark in South London in 1599, dismantling and then reassembling their previous theatre building, The Theatre, on the new site and calling it Globe Theatre, Kemp was still part of the company. The Lord Chamberlain's Men was a collective enterprise, owned by a handful of actor-sharers (which included one in-house dramatist, Shakespeare), all of whom were involved in the financial venture of the Globe, contributing to its costs in return for a share of the profits. It is not known why Kemp sold his share to the other partners and left the troupe in 1600, first striking out as a solo entertainer, whose most famous stunt was to dance all the way from London to Norwich, on which he capitalised in a published account, *Nine Daies Wonder* (1600), and then joining the Worcester's Men at the Curtain, a company that staged plays with a more radically Protestant slant than Shakespeare's company.[17]

The new comic lead at the Globe, Robert Armin, was a comedian of quite another sort.[18] It is difficult to imagine a more striking contrast to his predecessor. Where Kemp was athletic and of imposing stage presence, Armin was diminutive and ungainly, and mined his unprepossessing appearance for comedic value. Where Kemp's roles were built around the persona of a plain-talking buffoon, who frequently stumbles over linguistic obstacles, Armin's fools are razor-sharp in their wit, revelling in riddles, quibbles, and paradox. In *Twelfth Night*, Feste calls himself a professional 'corrupter of words' (3.1.31). And while Kemp presented himself as a man of the people, cultivating a close relationship with the spectators, with whom he shared a distanced perspective on the world of the high-born characters, Armin's fools are loners, outsiders with regard to both the audience and the play world.

Armin laid claim to a strain of intellectual humour, displayed in his works, *Quips upon Questions* and *Fool upon Fool* (both 1600), and disdained Will Kemp's brand of buffoonery. In *As You Like It*, Touchstone engages in a double act with a yokel named William, who prides himself on his 'pretty wit'. Touchtone remarks caustically, 'I do now remember a saying: "The fool doth think he is wise, but the wise man knows himself to be a fool"' (5.1.26–9). William is courting the uncouth country wench Audrey, but the superior comedian runs witty circles around his competitor and sends him packing. Translating simple words of French origin into even simpler ones, which he claims are the only sort a bumpkin will understand, he concludes mockingly: 'Therefore, you clown, abandon—which is in the vulgar "leave"—the society—which in the boorish is "company"—of this female—which in the common is "woman"' (42–5). The clown is unceremoniously asked to vacate the stage in favour of his far more nimble-witted successor. The joke has been adapted as a running gag for the spoof Shakespearean sit-com *Upstart Crow*, created by comedian Ben Elton and with fellow comic Spencer Jones playing the in-house comic (here called Kempe) as a caricature of celebrity comedian Ricky Gervais. Jones apes Gervais' abrasive mannerisms and is quite insufferable, constantly lecturing his fellow actors about the art of comedy: 'Test the boundaries, challenge the form, yeah?' Where Gervais is apt to remind his peers of his celebrity status abroad, particularly in America, in *Upstart Crow* Kempe smugly reminds his long-suffering colleagues that he is 'big in Italy'.[19] For comedians, the number one hobby at all times is scoffing at other comedians.

Shakespeare probably developed his wise fools, characters like Touchstone in *As You Like It*, Feste in *Twelfth Night*, Lavatch in *All's Well That Ends Well*, and the Fool in *King Lear*, in close collaboration with Armin.[20] But equally important in shaping the figure of the wise fool is the influence of Erasmus' satirical masterpiece, *Praise of Folly*. Written in 1509 and dedicated to his friend, Sir Thomas More—the original Latin title, *Moriae Encomium*, is a pun on More's name, playing on the Greek for 'folly'—it was published in 1511 and continually revised up to the edition of 1532. The second edition of 1515, produced by the famous Basle humanist and printer, Johannes Froben, who became Erasmus' favourite publisher, appeared with marginal illustrations by Hans Holbein the Younger. The little volume became an instant bestseller. By the time Erasmus died in 1536, thirty-six editions had appeared. The text was translated into English by Thomas Chaloner in 1549.[21] The book became famous for its satire of contemporary society, which Erasmus, in a sweeping indictment of scholars, lawyers, philosophers, theologians, princes, courtiers, and men of the cloth, depicts as a motley bunch of fools. But what makes the book unique and sets it apart from other fool literature (works like Sebastian Brant's *Ship of Fools*, which appeared in 1496) which castigates different ranks and professions, taking aim at their vanity and social aspirations, is the fact that it is soaked in self-deprecating irony.

Both Erasmus and More were enthusiastic about Lucian, the second-century BC Greek satirist whose send-up of superstition warmed the cockles of their humanist hearts; they produced a joint volume of translations of his work into Latin. Lucian's mastery of the mock encomium, a classical genre that delivered praise of an unworthy subject—there were mock encomia in praise of the gnat, the fly, baldness, quartan fever, and the parasite—was influential in the resurgence of the style in the Renaissance. Erasmus' innovation was to have the personification of Folly deliver a eulogy to herself.[22] The effect is to undercut everything she says, setting off a vertiginous spiral of ambiguities.

At the time, the term 'folly' encompassed a spectrum of connotations extending from foolishness to insanity.[23] As Folly remarks sardonically, folly is universal: 'I doubt if a single individual could be found from the whole of mankind who is wise every hour of his life and doesn't suffer from some form of insanity. The only difference is one of degree.'[24] Folly distinguishes men's lust for war and thirst for wealth from more benign forms of madness like delusion, self-love, and ignorance. These, she claims facetiously, are nothing but a blessing in disguise. No marriage would last if it were not built on the foundation of self-deception, no friendship would survive without turning a blind eye to one another's faults. Civil society is grounded on mutual flattery. Self-delusion makes for happiness: we *want* to be deceived. Folly takes classical precepts and distorts them, creating a mélange of sense and nonsense.[25] Drawing on the theatrical imagery that runs throughout the text, Folly insists, 'To destroy the illusion is to ruin the whole play.' She ruminates, 'Now, what else is the whole life of man but a sort of play? Actors come on wearing their different masks and all play their parts' (44). Real folly is to ask 'for the play to stop being a play'. Illusion is indispensable for the games we play: 'this is the way to play the comedy of life' (45). Erasmus' own little in-joke was that despite her cavils at the austere Stoics, who turn a deaf ear to her appeal to indulge in the pleasures of life, Folly is happy to resort to the Stoic commonplace of life as a stage.[26]

While Folly's bantering tone turns increasingly acid when she describes the superstitions and follies of Erasmus' contemporaries, in the last section of the book she turns to the key paradox in the text: Christ too was a fool, she avers. We are all fools in the eyes of God; by becoming human, Christ joined the multitude of fools, however briefly. Citing St Paul's ironic remark to the Corinthians, 'We are fools for Christ's sake' (1 Cor. 4:10, *KJV*), in which he compares the comfortable lifestyle of the fledgling Christian community at Corinth to the hardship endured by the apostles, Folly triumphantly enlists the founder of the Church as her disciple. However impish his tone, Erasmus is making a serious point, laced with more than a trace of self-mockery. All quest for human knowledge is vanity in relation to the wisdom of God. And those who live a life of piety and decline to pursue goals like wealth or status are derided as fools by the rest of humanity. In order to gain spiritual wisdom, a true believer would need to become a fool by worldly standards. Or as Paul puts it, 'If any man among you seemeth to be wise in this world, let him become a fool, that he may be wise' (1 Cor. 3:18, KJV).

What Shakespeare absorbed from Erasmus' *jeu d'esprit* is the tone of wry amusement which permeates the text. He also borrowed the notion that fools are not other people, but ourselves. His wise fools hold up a mirror to the rest of us, implicitly posing the question, 'Who is the real fool?' Often, they are merely interested in verbal quibbles, spinning out pointless puns ad infinitum. But sometimes there is a nugget of wisdom hidden in the dross. They are outsiders, observing the absurd goings-on in the main plot with distanced irony, not because of their low social status, as is the case with the clowns, but because they are usually loners, without close ties to any other character. Above all, they are professional entertainers. And like Folly, the wise fools are partial to games of self-reference, foregrounding their own status as performers—and everyone else's too, both onstage and in the audience.

In *As You Like It*, the court jester Touchstone finds himself stranded in the middle of a pastoral idyll, the forest of Arden. He promptly sets about to undermine the genre from within. In a comic duo with the shepherd Corin, who plays straight man to Touchstone's funny man, the fool proceeds to deploy chop logic to demolish the bromides the denizen of the forest has just spouted: 'that the property of rain is to wet and fire to burn; that good pasture makes fat sheep and that a great cause of the night is the lack of the sun' (3.2.24–5). Having ascertained that the shepherd has never been at court, Touchstone announces categorically that he is damned. When asked to explain what he means, he declares, 'if thou never wast at court thou never saw'st good manners. If thou never saw'st good manners, then thy manners must be wicked, and wickedness is sin, and sin is damnation', wrapping up dramatically, 'Thou art in parlous state, shepherd!' (36–9). Touchstone is quibbling on the multiple meanings of the word 'manners', which in early modern English could refer to polite comportment, to customary modes of behaviour, or to morality.[27] Uncowed, Corin protests that different codes of conduct apply in different surroundings. One instance is the courtly habit of kissing hands. This would be unthinkable in the country, he contends, where shepherds' hands are greasy and tarred from handling their sheep, whereas courtiers' hands are perfumed with civet musk. Touchstone will have none of it. Civet, he lectures the rustic, 'is of baser birth than tar—the very uncleanly flux of a cat', referring to the origin of musk in animal anal glands (59). He also gives short shrift to Corin's sententious pronouncement, 'I earn that I eat, get that I wear, owe no man hate, envy no man's happiness . . . and the greatest of my pride is to see my ewes graze and my lambs suck' (64–7). Corin is nothing but a bawd, Touchstone insists, living 'by the copulation of cattle' (69–70). Touchstone is keen to put down the shepherd, invariably the subject of romantic idealisation in pastoral literature, and quashes his intimation of a lost Golden Age of peace and harmony by comparing his line of work to that of a pimp. But at the same time, the fool takes a side-swipe at courtiers, hinting at less savoury descriptions of climbing the greasy pole. For spectators, the comic routine would evoke an additional source of ironic humour: the idyll of pastoral life was a fiction, invented by courtiers for courtiers. It had nothing at all to do with the reality of the countryside.

Touchstone also debunks another literary fiction in the play: Petrarchan love. He parodies Orlando's love poetry with bawdy doggerel of his own: 'If the cat will after kind,/So, be sure, will Rosalind' (92–3). He uses a similarly debased analogy to defend his wholly unromantic relationship with the dim-witted Audrey: 'As the ox hath his bow, sir, the horse his curb, and the falcon her bells, so man hath his desires' (3.3.67–8). Nonetheless, he joins the queue to be married, 'amongst the rest of country copulatives' (5.4.53). Touchstone is both detached observer and participant in the play; to this extent he differs from Feste, possibly the most Erasmian of the wise fools.

Take, for instance, Feste's catechising of Olivia, set on mourning her brother for a period of seven years:

> Clown: Good madonna, why mourn'st thou?
> Olivia: Good fool, for my brother's death.
> Clown: I think his soul is in hell, madonna.
> Olivia: I know his soul is in heaven, fool.
> Clown: The more fool, madonna, to mourn for your brother's
> soul, being in heaven. Take away the fool, gentlemen.
> (*Twelfth Night* 1.5.59–64)

Twelfth Night is a play about shades of folly. As Feste notes drily, Illyria is teeming with fools: 'Foolery . . . does walk about the orb like the sun. It shines everywhere' (3.1.33–4). Far from chastising the Illyrians, he uses sleight of logic, as in the dialogue above, to lay bare their folly. Despite her morbid fascination with mourning, he suggests, Olivia is not really grieving for the death of her brother. Instead, she is wrapped in a cocoon of self-absorption and delusion. Of the two of them, she is the greater fool. Whether Olivia grasps the point he is making remains unclear. Perhaps Viola, herself an outsider and role-player, is the only character who fully appreciates the subtle art involved in acting the fool. 'This fellow is wise enough to play the fool', she muses in terms that resonate with Erasmian paradox. The fool must have a firm insight into human psychology: 'He must observe their mood on whom he jests,/ The quality of persons, and the time' (3.1.55–6). A consummate professional, adept at slipping in and out of roles, as Feste's parody of the vacuous parson, Sir Topas, shows, the fool's jesting is carefully calibrated to his audience.

Viola's admiration for Feste is not reciprocated. The fool tells her coolly, 'I do not care for you' (26). There is little sense that Feste cares for anyone at all. His main interest lies in persuading his aristocratic punters to part with their small change. At times, he evinces a decidedly callous streak. In the gulling of Malvolio, disguised as Sir Topas, he seems to enjoy goading the distraught steward, driving him to the brink of insanity, although he is careful to fulfil his request for paper and ink.[28] Earlier in the play, Malvolio disparages the quality of his humour, but there is no mention of reprisals towards the fool for delivering unvarnished truths. On the contrary: Olivia defends his licence to speak his mind, insisting, 'There is no slander in an allowed fool' (1.5.85–6). There is, however, a price to be paid: the wise fool is not taken seriously. In the final analysis, he is merely an entertainer whose value lies in the way he packages his truths. What counts is the media, not the message. No one is more aware of this than Feste himself. As he notes in his valedictory song, in the face of 'the wind and the rain', his role is to provide diversion: 'we'll strive to please you every day' (5.1.376; 393–94).

SPEAKING TRUTH TO POWER

Possibly, the successors to the wise fools in contemporary society are the late-night show hosts in US television, whose satirical shows are watched by millions of viewers throughout the world. Comedians like Stephen Colbert of *The Late Show with Stephen Colbert*, Trevor Noah of *The Daily Show*, and John Oliver of *Last Week Tonight* regularly skewer those in power. Colbert became famous for *The Colbert Report* (2005–14), a programme in which he plays self-referential games with a character named 'Stephen Colbert', the parodic version of a right-wing media personality. In an ironic twist, the views he voiced in character were frequently taken at face value by conservative viewers. In the meantime, Trevor Noah, successor to the legendary Jon Stewart, often seen as the moral conscience of liberal America, has carved out a persona for himself that is reminiscent of Shakespeare's wise fools, hovering on the borders of society and commenting on the follies of its members with amused detachment (Figure 3.1). As an outsider in American society, South African by birth, he is ideally situated for the role of embedded observer; as a person of mixed ethnic descent—his father is Swiss, his mother a black South African—he straddles the divide between white and black.

Figure 3.1 *The Daily Show* (2019), Dir. Paul Pennolino, produced by Comedy Central

Noah exploits his position on the boundaries between social and racial worlds for comedy gold. A typical joke turns on the myths that races and nations fondly nurture about each other. He describes how after his shows, black Americans regularly come up to him and tell him about their hopes of relocating to Africa. This, they believe, is where they will find their authentic self. Ironically, once Trump's presidency was imminent, the comedian found himself assailed by white Americans who wanted to move to Africa to escape the new regime.[29] Noah does not savage either of these groups. Instead, he gently mocks the illusions they cling to and the dreams they hanker after, which are, in fact, modern versions of the pastoral myth of the Golden Age that Touchstone takes apart in *As You Like It*. Noah is as canny as Feste in retailing his comic wares and recycling them to suit his ends. The same joke is pressed into service as a joke about South African politics. When after decades of apartheid the transition to majority rule took place, white South Africans were keen to move away to escape the horrors of living in a society with black Africans in power. They dreamed of relocating to Australia. Their fears were allayed by Nelson Mandela's policy of reconciliation. When the wildly erratic demagogue Jacob Zuma came to power, it was the turn of black South Africans to look for ways to escape the conditions in their country—once again, by dreaming of a life elsewhere, preferably in Australia.[30] In our age, Australia has taken the place of Arcadia, a site where we believe reinventing ourselves is still possible.

Shakespeare too repackages Feste's song about the wind and the rain and has the Fool sing it in *King Lear* (3.2.74–7).[31] If *Twelfth Night* is a study in folly, *King Lear* probes the most radical connotations of the term. It portrays a world swept up in a maelstrom of madness. In the first act of the play, the Fool is tireless in his efforts to lay bare the hubris and self-delusion in which the King is mired. When the banished Kent returns in disguise, asking to be taken into service with Lear, the Fool gives him the mocking advice to don the garb of a jester. In truth, the camouflaged jibe is directed at the King, who takes the bait. When Lear asks why the Fool demands that Kent wear a coxcomb, the swift response is: 'for taking one's part that's out of favour'. The Fool turns to Kent and explains, 'Why, this fellow has banished two on's daughters and did the third a blessing against his will. If thou follow him, thou must needs wear my coxcomb' (1.4.91–5). In other words, only a fool would serve a king who has made the fatal decisions that Lear has. But like all the wise fools, Lear's Fool scrambles truth with nonsense, speaking in riddles. To speak of a king as being 'out of favour' is patently absurd, although it contains a barbed truth: Lear has wilfully reduced himself to the status of a retainer of his daughters and is dependent on their favour. And as for Cordelia, although the Fool is right that by revoking her dowry, Lear indirectly did her a favour, winnowing the wheat from the chaff among her suitors, this might not as yet be clear to the King. Furthermore, Lear has just banished one daughter, not two. Characteristically, the truths delivered by the fool are hedged about with a disclaimer: this is just foolery. Any resemblance to living kings is purely coincidental.

The Fool sharpens his comparison between Lear and a fool throughout the scene. In a comic set piece dripping with irony, he juggles simultaneously with the meanings of the word 'crown' (a symbol of royalty, the head), a jestbook fable, and the paradoxes of wisdom and folly.

Fool: Nuncle, give me an egg, and I'll give thee two crowns.
Lear: What two crowns shall they be?

> Fool: Why, after I have cut the egg i'th' middle and ate up the
> meat, the two crowns of the egg. When thou clovest
> thy crown i'th' middle and gav'st away both parts, thou
> bor'st thine ass on thy back o'er the dirt. Thou hadst
> little wit in thy bald crown when thou gav'st thy golden
> one away. If I speak like myself in this, let him be
> whipped that first finds it so.
>
> (*The Tragedy of King Lear*, 1.4.128–35)

The Fool creates the satirical effect he is aiming for by deploying bathos: debasing kingship to an egg. But it is Lear, he
implies, who is responsible for the degradation of royal
authority by dividing the kingdom and distributing the parts
to his daughters. As in the fable of the old man who, to please
those who criticised him for overburdening his donkey, carried the beast on his back, Lear has made a fool of himself,
becoming a universal laughing stock.[32] The Fool baldly labels
the King a fool—only to defuse his insolence by reminding
his listeners that he is merely a fool. However, there is a sting
in the tail of his disclaimer too. The layered ambiguities leave
it unclear whether he is claiming he was telling the truth after
all, but that anyone who admitted as much would be punished, or whether he is urging that anyone who believes he
is being foolish in his assertion that the King is the real fool
should be punished for their blindness to the truth.

The 'all-licensed fool' (168) escapes being disciplined for
his audacity, although the King does warn him he might
be whipped, leading the jester to complain that he is being
bullied from all sides: the daughters threaten to have him
whipped 'for speaking true', and the king 'for lying' (152–3).
Given the proximity of the wise fool to figures of authority,
whether in a great house or at court, one of the questions the

plays explore is the relationship between humour and power. The question remains one of perennial interest. In Armando Iannucci's dark satire, *The Death of Stalin*, the members of the Central Committee are depicted competing with each other to ply the dictator with jokes at dinner (Figure 3.2).[33] When Nikita Khrushchev returns home at night, his wife meticulously notes down the jokes that worked. And those that didn't. The wrong joke might mean that his name would be added to the list of the next day's purges. Ironically, the film was banned in Russia for allegedly insulting Soviet history.

Precisely how effective is humour as a political tool? In dictatorships, humour is often fraught with danger—the Nazi state meted out death sentences to joke tellers, while tens of thousands were sent to the Gulag in Stalinist joke-trials. In Soviet Russia in 1934, an official campaign to propagate 'positive humour' was initiated, which implied encouraging benign, cheerful jokes about Communist society and reserving satire for the enemies of the state.[34] Nonetheless, an underground

Figure 3.2 *The Death of Stalin* (2017), Dir. Armando Iannucci, produced by Gaumont, Quad Productions, Main Journey, France 3 Cinema, La Cie Cinématographique, Panache Productions, AFPI, Canal+, Ciné+, France Télévisions, Title Media

culture of anti-Communist jokes flourished throughout Eastern Europe. In the face of the repression of jokes in tyrannical regimes, humour is widely regarded as a subversive force, undermining power from within. The Shakespearean wise fools, modelled on court fools in the absolutist regimes of Europe, mock the follies of their powerful patrons. By uncovering their weaknesses, they puncture the arrogance and self-assurance of the ruling class.

Or so we believe. Some critics, however, are more sceptical. They argue that far from undermining a regime, humour serves to shore up its authority. Showing how flawed the ruling class is only underscores the naked truth that they *are* the ruling class. It is a demonstration of power. This might explain why tyrants have been fond of maintaining a truth-telling jester in their entourage.[35] In a study of jokes under Communism, Ben Lewis suggests that joke tellers might have been persecuted less for their jokes than to send a message that the state would not tolerate even the smallest trace of opposition. He also points out that Stalin often laughed at the same jokes about himself that were circulating underground.[36] For a dictator, humour about his cruelty and arbitrary wielding of power might translate as flattery. (Presumably, Stalin would have enjoyed *The Death of Stalin*.) The satirical British puppet show *Spitting Image* was avidly watched by politicians. John O'Farrell, a lead writer for the show, recalls how he was importuned by Members of Parliament to include them in the show. However much they might be lampooned, it was far worse to be ignored by the famous satirical programme.[37]

One might also argue that for the segment of society in opposition to the established rulers, jokes can defuse anger and frustration. The entertainment factor in satire can undercut the didactic point it is making. As a safety valve for righteous outrage, humour can deflect the impetus to take action, reducing opposition to small-scale resistance. It might even foster a cynical stance, eroding any interest in changing the status quo. What is more, satire preaches to the converted. The audiences watching late-night shows are the same members of the (predominantly East coast) chattering classes who rejected Trump as a vulgar upstart from the very start. Perhaps the myth of the subversive power of humour is another of our cherished illusions, akin to the nostalgia for the Golden Age that Touchstone mocks or the dream of an authentic homeland elsewhere that Noah pokes fun at.

Satirists themselves are less starry-eyed about the power of humour. The British comedian Peter Cook lauded the cabaret of the Weimar Republic as the greatest satire of the twentieth century, given its success in preventing the rise of Hitler.[38] Colbert too disavows any claims that satire is an effective political instrument. Comedy, he states, allows spectators (and himself) to experience a rush of happiness; after his show, 'maybe the audience sleeps a bit better'.[39] Trevor Noah alleges that comedy is not about the arguments you make, but about making people think. But he also defends comedy as a means to build bridges between people and to 'spur conversations'.[40] It is true that shared humour creates a sense of community— although mainly among those who belong to the same political spectrum. As regards its political effect, the jury is still out.

Humour might make nothing happen, but it can serve as a strategy of survival. When Lear's Fool discovers Kent in the stocks, he repeats his advice to quit the service of a king headed for disaster: 'Let go thy hold when a great wheel runs down a hill, lest it break thy neck with following. But the great one that goes upward, let him draw thee after' (2.2.251–54). He urges Kent to switch his allegiance to someone whose star is in the ascendant. For all his corrosive humour, the Fool himself stays loyal to the King, although, as the play hints, it costs him dear. When Lear storms out into the wind and the rain, only the Fool follows him, 'who labours to out-jest/His heart-struck injuries' (3.1.8–9). In an increasingly dark play, the Fool adapts his humour to Lear's fate, jesting to shore against his ruins.

NOTES

1 T. S. Eliot, 'The Love Song of J. Alfred Prufrock', *The Norton Anthology of Poetry*, ed. Margaret Ferguson et al., 4th ed. (New York: W. W. Norton, 1996), 1232, line 111.

2 Ibid., 1233, lines 118–19.

3 David Wiles, *Shakespeare's Clown: Actor and Text in the Elizabethan Playhouse* (Cambridge: Cambridge University Press, 1987), and Bart van Es, *Shakespeare in Company* (Oxford: Oxford University Press, 2013). In the following I draw on their work.

4 On Tarlton, see Andrew Gurr, *Playgoing in Shakespeare's England*, 3rd ed. (Cambridge: Cambridge University Press, 2004), 150–58, and Wiles, *Shakespeare's Clown*, 11–23.

5 On Tarlton as a national star, see Alexander Halasz, 'So Beloved that Men Use His Picture for their Signs', *Shakespeare Studies* 23 (1995): 19–38, and Richard Helgerson, *Forms of Nationhood: The Elizabethan Writing of England* (Chicago: University of Chicago Press, 1992), 215–28.

6 See Gurr, *Playgoing in Shakespeare's England*, 158.

7 See Wiles, *Shakespeare's Clown*, 43–60, and Gurr, *Playgoing in Shakespeare's England*, 182–83.

8 Philosopher Simon Critchley explains that humans laugh at animal jokes because they make us aware of our precarious position between animal and non-animal. See Critchley, *On Humour* (London: Routledge, 2002), 25–38.

9 Two valuable studies of the play are William C. Carroll, *The Great Feast of Language in Love's Labour's Lost* (Princeton, NJ: Princeton University Press, 1976) and Louis Adrian Montrose, '*Curious-knotted Garden': The Form, Themes, and Contexts of Shakespeare's Love's Labour's Lost* (Salzburg: Institut für Englische Sprache und Literatur, Universität Salzburg, 1977).

10 A foundational work is Enid Welsford's *The Fool: His Social and Literary History* (London: Faber and Faber, 1935). Recent studies include Robert

Hornback, *The English Clown Tradition from the Middle Ages to Shakespeare* (Cambridge: D. S. Brewer, 2009), Robert H. Bell, *Shakespeare's Great Stage of Fools* (New York: Palgrave Macmillan, 2011), and Robert Preiss, *Clowning and Authorship in Early Modern Theatre* (Oxford: Oxford University Press, 2014).

11 Jonathan Swift, *Gulliver's Travels*, ed. Claude Rawson, Oxford World's Classics (Oxford: Oxford University Press, 2005), 97. Italics in the original. All further references in parentheses.

12 *Borat: Cultural Learning of America for Make Benefit Glorious Nation of Kazakhstan*, dir. Larry Charles, perf. Sacha Baron Cohen, Ken Davitian (20th Century Fox, 2006) and *Borat Subsequent Moviefilm: Delivery of Prodigious Bribe to American Regime for Make Benefit Once Glorious Nation of Kazakhstan*, dir. Jason Woliner, perf. Sacha Baron Cohen, Maria Bakalova (Amazon Studios, 2020).

13 See www.nytimes.com/2018/06/04/us/politics/supreme-court-sides-with-baker-who-turned-away-gay-couple.html.

14 See www.insider.com/borat-2-macy-chanel-interview-2020-10.

15 Jonathan Swift, 'Preface', in *The Battle of the Books* (1704), K2v.

16 In the quarto version of *Much Ado About Nothing*, published in 1600, a number of Dogberry's speeches appear with Kemp's name attached, providing valuable evidence that Shakespeare wrote roles to the requirements of the actors of the troupe. See Trudi Darby, 'Textual Introduction', *Much Ado About Nothing, The Norton Shakespeare: Comedies*, 531.

17 On Kemp see Wiles, *Shakespeare's Clown*, 24–42.

18 On Armin, see in particular Wiles, *Shakespeare's Clown*, 136–63, and van Es, *Shakespeare in Company*, 163–94.

19 *Upstart Crow*, Season 1, Episodes 1 and 3.

20 A classic study of the wise fool is Robert Hillis Goldsmith, *Wise Fools in Shakespeare* (East Lansing, MI: Michigan University Press, 1955).

21 A. H. T. Levi, 'Introduction', in *Praise of Folly and Letter to Maarten Van Dorp 1515*, by Desiderius Erasmus, trans. Betty Radice, Penguin Classics (London: Penguin Book, 1993), xii. Valuable readings of *Praise of Folly* are provided by Walter Kaiser, *Praisers of Folly: Erasmus, Rabelais, Shakespeare* (Cambridge, MA: Harvard University Press, 1963) and Rosalie L. Colie, *Paradoxia Epidemica: The Renaissance Tradition of Paradox* (Princeton, NJ: Princeton University Press, 1966).

22 Erika Michael points out that even among classical mock encomia, texts in which the subjects are the speakers themselves are very rare. One example is Lucian's oration allegedly delivered by the tyrant Phalaris,

who sings his own praises. See Erika Michael, *The Drawings by Hans Holbein the Younger for Erasmus' 'Praise of Folly'* (New York: Garland, 1986), 21.

23 See 'folly, n.1', *Oxford English Dictionary Online*.

24 *Praise of Folly*, 60. All further references in parentheses.

25 See W. David Kay, 'Erasmus' Learned Joking: The Ironic Use of Classical Wisdom in *The Praise of Folly*', *Texas Studies in Literature and Language* 19.3 (1977): 247–67.

26 The Stoic philosopher Epictetus is cited as saying, 'Remember that you are an actor in a play . . . this is your business, to play admirably the rôle assigned you'. See Epictetus, *The Encheiridion*, trans. W. A. Oldfather, Loeb Classical Library (Cambridge, MA: Harvard University Press, 1928), 17.

27 'manner, n.', 4, *Oxford English Dictionary Online*.

28 See A. C. Bradley, 'Feste the Jester', in *Shakespeare: Twelfth Night*, ed. D. J. Palmer, Casebook Series (London: Macmillan, 1972), 63–71; rpt. from *A Book of Homage to Shakespeare* (Oxford: Oxford University Press, 1916).

29 Trevor Noah, *You Laugh But It's True*, dir. David Paul Meyer (Netflix, 2011).

30 *Trevor Noah: Afraid of the Dark*, dir. David Paul Meyer (Netflix, 2017).

31 *The Tragedy of King Lear*, in *The Norton Shakespeare: Tragedies*.

32 See notes to William Shakespeare, *King Lear*, ed. R. A. Foakes, The Arden Shakespeare, third series (London: Thomson Learning, 1997).

33 *The Death of Stalin*, dir. Armando Iannucci (Gaumont, 2017).

34 See Ben Lewis, *Hammer and Tickle: The History of Communism Told Through Communist Jokes* (London: Weidenfeld & Nicolson, 2008), 40–44.

35 Anton C. Zijderveld, *Reality in a Looking-Glass: Rationality Through an Analysis of Traditional Folly* (London: Routledge & Kegan Paul, 1982), 27–30. On humour and politics, also see Andrew Stott, *Comedy*, The New Critical Idiom (New York: Routledge, 2005), 103–26, and Terry Eagleton, 'The Politics of Humour', in *Humour* (New Haven, CT: Yale University Press, 2019), 136–64.

36 See Lewis, *Hammer and Tickle*, 75, 54.

37 www.theguardian.com/tv-and-radio/2020/oct/01/spitting-image-satire-ian-hislop-roy-hattersley

38 www.independent.co.uk/news/people/obituary-peter-cook-1567341.html

39 www.nytimes.com/interactive/2019/06/03/magazine/stephen-colbert-politics-religion.html

40 www.theguardian.com/stage/2019/jul/13/trevor-noah-on-satires-uphill-battle-in-the-age-of-trump-the-daily-show

Four

'Wit larded with malice'

Troilus and Cressida 5.1.50

A scene that is not usually listed among Shakespeare's funny interludes is a brief episode in *Julius Caesar*. Mark Antony has just addressed the crowd gathered to watch him pay his respects to Caesar. In a blaze of oratory, he has successfully stirred them up and unleashed an orgy of destruction. While the crowd chants, 'Revenge! About! Seek! Burn! Fire! Kill! Slay!' (3.2.202), Antony gloats, 'Mischief, thou art afoot;/Take thou what course thou wilt' (258–9). Enter a bit-part character, Cinna the poet. He barely has time to tell the audience that he has had a bad night, filled with ominous dreams, before the mob surround him and fire off a salvo of questions at him.

First Plebeian:	What is your name?
Second Plebeian:	Whither are you going?
Third Plebeian:	Where do you dwell?
Fourth Plebeian:	Are you a married man or a bachelor?

(3.3.5–8)

The inquiries are banal, the tone menacing. When the bemused Cinna tells them he is a bachelor, one of his inquisitors

DOI: 10.4324/9780429317507-5

threatens him with violence for allegedly insinuating 'they are fools that marry' (17–8). And although Cinna insists he is of the party of Caesar, his name triggers an outburst of rage. He shares the same name as one of Caesar's assassins.

First Plebeian: Tear him to pieces! He's a conspirator.
Cinna: I am Cinna the poet, I am Cinna the poet!
Fourth Plebeian: Tear him for his bad verses, tear him for his
                   bad verses!

(3.5.27–30)

There is no question of the crowd mistaking his identity; they know perfectly well that the man in front of them is not guilty of conspiring against Caesar. They do not care. The scene is a demonstration of the lethal power inherent in rhetoric, and a first taste of the chaos into which Rome will descend, evoked by Antony in his ominous vow to 'Cry havoc and let slip the dogs of war' (3.1.275). It is also a parodic replay of the assassination of Caesar. Here the plebeians ape the acts of their betters and massacre a man for having the wrong name. In a recent production set in South Africa, the crowd is shown 'necklacing' the victim, a pastime in which a mob puts a tyre around the neck of an alleged traitor or police informer and sets it on fire, made notorious by Winnie Mandela in the 1980s and 1990s during the struggle against the South African apartheid regime.[1]

What is sometimes overlooked is that for all its horror, the scene is also wildly funny. It is an example of the type of black humour with which Shakespeare's tragedies are suffused, in which horrifying moments are presented in a jesting manner.[2] The humour resides not just in the sadistic pleasure of bullying a hapless victim, but in the incongruity of the breathtaking triviality of the reasons put forward for punishing a patently innocent citizen and for the cruelty meted out to him. One plebeian proposes, 'Pluck but the name out of his heart, and turn him going' (32–3), cynically suggesting that someone could be purged of the ostensible crime of their name by ripping them apart. For a brief, Daliesque moment, a surreal image of dismembered humans flashes in front of us, which, however ghastly, is quite hilarious in its absurdity. The farcical violence of scenes like this offers a distorted image of the horrendous reality that it mirrors, sharpening our dulled senses to perceive the absurdities of the world in which we live and which we have made.

There is a further layer to this grim joke. Shakespeare's main source for the play was Plutarch's *Life of Julius Caesar*, which describes Cinna as a friend of Caesar's. But for his depiction of the scene, Shakespeare draws on another account, the *Life of Marcus Brutus*, where Cinna is named as a poet.[3] Shakespeare turns the way we savage a writer for the poor quality of his work into a literal image, adding a touch of self-parody to the joke. Why Shakespeare should underline the idea that Cinna is a poet is open to debate. Perhaps, as has been argued, he is warning poets with a more overtly political agenda not to meddle with politics—fellow-playwrights Ben Jonson and George Chapman were briefly imprisoned in 1605 for anti-Scottish satire in their play *Eastward Ho*, taken amiss by Scotsman James I.[4] After his ill-advised laudatory words about the Earl of Essex in *Henry V*, the play written immediately before *Julius Caesar*, in which the Chorus contemplates the loving welcome that London would offer Essex when he returns victorious from crushing the rebels in Ireland (5.0.29–34), Shakespeare himself was never to make a direct allusion to contemporary politics again. (Essex slunk back to London after a disastrous campaign and was executed not long after for plotting to overthrow the Queen.)[5] Or perhaps Shakespeare is making a wry comment on the inescapable embroilment of art in power struggles, however much a writer might wish to evade them.[6] But quite apart from Shakespeare's little in-joke, the scene lays bare our own entanglement in the culture of cruelty it presents: our perfect willingness to enjoy violence and inhumanity if served with a large dollop of humour. This is as true of his spectators as of us today. At the same time as gratifying our pleasure in the ludicrous, dark humour elicits an uneasy sense that we might be a part of the world we deplore and share the barbaric impulses we are laughing at. It creates a sneaking suspicion that the real joke is on us.[7]

MALEVOLENT JESTERS

In 2016, a wave of creepy clowns dominated the news. Pranksters dressed up as evil clowns were sighted across the United States and the UK, and set off a hysteria at schools and in social media. A spurt of copycat sinister-clown incidents was reported all over the world. This was not the first time that a panic had emerged around the rumoured sightings of menacing clowns. Organisations like the World Clown Association and Clowns International, the oldest clown club in the world, felt it incumbent on them to protest, pointing out that real clowns were benign entertainers whose only aim was to please.[8] This might be the case for their members, but in truth, clowns have been ambiguous figures in many cultures, and since ancient times. The equation of clowns with good clean fun is a Victorian invention, in the same way as the sad Pierrot is largely a Romantic invention.[9] Long before that, in medieval Europe, associating clowning with malevolence was a deep-rooted tradition. The main dramatic form during the late medieval period, the morality play, featured a trickster figure who evolved into the star of the stage—the Vice. Originally a servant of the Devil, he took the guise of a number of pernicious traits (and was variously named Hypocrisy, Mischief, or Iniquity). The plots are dominated by the Vice attempting to seduce an Everyman figure from the path of virtue. But his main function is to provide merriment to the audience. Bursting with vitality, incessantly engaged in high jinx, he keeps up a stream of comic patter to the spectators, gleefully commenting on his success in manipulating his victims. His greatest pleasure lies in malicious intrigue, purely for its own sake. First and foremost, the Vice was a comic entertainer.[10]

The tradition of grimly farcical humour and malignant jesters continued to influence drama in the early modern period. In *Doctor Faustus*, Christopher Marlowe produced a play exploring existential anguish which is interspersed with scenes of diabolical slapsick, while the main protagonist of *The Jew of Malta*, Barabas, is both a vicious schemer and a consummate comic showman. T. S. Eliot famously described *The Jew of Malta* as a farce, admitting that 'with the enfeebled humour of our times the word is a misnomer; it is the farce of the old English humour, the terribly serious, even savage comic humour, the humour which spent its last breath on the decadent genius of Dickens'.[11] The myth that humour is wholesome, like ice cream, a harmless pleasure we all enjoy, has always been undermined by swirling undercurrents of wildly cruel comedy. (Never mind that ice cream isn't benign either, on numerous counts, not least calorific ones.) The plays of Shakespeare's contemporaries are populated with sneering jesters, often in double acts with snarling malcontents (Carlo Buffone and Malicente in Ben Jonson's *Every Man Out of His Humour*, or Passarello and Malevole in John Marston's *The Malcontent*). Despite their railing and verbal violence, most of them are ineffectual, as are the clowns and wise fools looked at in the previous chapter. With a few exceptions—Thersites in *Troilus and Cressida*, Apemantus in *Timon of Athen*—Shakespeare himself generally avoids the genre of satire, in which these misanthropic jokers are most at home. Instead, he is keen to explore an altogether different question: what happens when a joker gets his hands on real power, as opposed to the power of the entertainer over his audiences? And how are they related to each other? As in the scene in *Julius Caesar*, where comedy and brutality are closely intertwined, Shakespeare looks at the way jesting is bound up with power in various constellations.

The sinister clown phenomenon is thought to have been inspired by the figure of the Joker in the comic book series *Batman*, created by Bob Kane, which first appeared in 1940 with DC Comics. The archenemy of the superhero, he is depicted as a maniacal character with a penchant for twisted, malevolent humour. Marked by a razor-sharp mind, he is driven by an insatiable desire for mayhem and destruction. In a graphic novel published in 1988, *The Killing Joke*, Alan Moore and Brian Bolland created a back story for the character as a failed comedian who turns insane. The book ends with his relating an absurd joke, fading out on the note of his hysterical laughter.[12] In Christopher Nolan's legendary super-hero film, *The Dark Knight*, the Joker is a criminal master-mind who holds the entire city to ransom (Figure 4.1). Played by actor Heath Ledger as a sociopathic jester, he calls himself 'an agent of chaos' who wants to overthrow the established order and whose aim is 'to burn everything down'.[13] He doesn't quite succeed, but revels in the chaos he unleashes with patent glee. A repellent yet riveting figure who exults in flamboyant gestures,

Figure 4.1 *The Dark Knight* (2008), Dir. Christopher Nolan, produced by Warner Bros. Pictures DC Comics, Legendary Pictures, Syncopy

he is fully aware of his effect on his peers. If the film appears remarkably prescient, its roots lie in the way Shakespeare adapts the malign jesters of medieval drama to fully-fleshed out characters, most notably with Gloucester in *Richard III*, Iago in *Othello*, and Edmund in *King Lear*, all of whose agendas prefigure that of the Joker in many ways. Theological issues about cosmic evil are transmuted to secular questions about the relationship between humour, power, and complicity.

THE GLAMOUR OF EVIL

Richard III sets off with a joke.[14] In a lengthy address to the audience, Richard, Duke of Gloucester, begins with the line, 'Now is the winter of our discontent'. Precisely when one would expect him to elucidate his lack of satisfaction with the times, he makes a volte-face, following up the first line with the words, 'Made glorious summer by this son of York' (1.1.1–2). Fooled you, he seems to crow—this is not a litany of woes at all. At the same time, the double syntax allows the hint of his dissatisfaction to hover in the air.[15] And contains a subtle threat: while it might seem that the second line is a tribute to his brother Edward, the newly crowned King Edward IV, the pun Richard uses is ambiguous. The play on the word 'son' (or 'sun') and the hackneyed image of a sun for kingship are unremarkable, but as Richard is slyly reminding us, he too is a son of the Duke of York. Richard manages to smuggle a little jest into the very first two lines of the play. But we are not the butt of the joke. On the contrary, he invites us to share it with him, seeming to select each and every one of us as a special invited guest. In truth, he is letting us into a secret. He might be mouthing platitudes in praise of the new regime, he insinuates, but to our ears only will he divulge the truth: he is discontented with the current state of affairs, but he will turn it to his advantage.

What Richard shares with the Vice of medieval drama is not just the spree of violence and destruction he embarks on, lying, deceiving, and murdering everyone who stands in his way, from his closest kin through staunch allies to children. Like the Vice, he is both main protagonist and commentator, straddling the world of the play and the world outside. He is also a brilliant comic entertainer. He goes to great lengths to draw the audience into his orbit, letting us in on his jokes and inviting us to chuckle along with him. He informs us in advance that he has set an intrigue in motion against his brother George, Duke of Clarence: 'Plots have I laid, inductions dangerous' (32). When Clarence, arrested at his instigation, enters under guard, Richard acts the solicitous brother: 'this deep disgrace in brotherhood/Touches me deeper than you can imagine' (111–12), he proclaims indignantly. What on one level sounds like an expression of concern, on another level, aimed at the audience, is a contemptuous jibe at his brother, revelling in the latter's ignorance of his machinations. We know, of course, that the arrest 'touches' or is a concern of Richard's in quite a different sense than Clarence might believe. A few lines later Richard promises his brother solemnly, 'I will deliver you or lie for you' (115), once again juggling with a variety of different meanings. Sanctimoniously assuring Clarence that he will work ceaselessly to secure his release, Richard winds up with the extravagant pledge that should he fail, he himself will take his brother's place in prison. At the same time, playing on the meaning of 'deliver' as 'to hand over', and with a wink aimed specifically at his spectators, he is making a veiled threat to deliver Clarence to a less salutary fate, and is boasting of his finesse in lying. Richard explicitly draws attention to his affinities with the Vice, one of whose traits is a skill at witty equivocation: 'like the formal Vice, Iniquity,/I moralize two meanings in one word' (3.1.82–3), he brags. And when Clarence is led away, Richard turns to us and smirks. 'Simple, plain Clarence, I do love thee so/That I will shortly send thy soul to heaven,/ If heaven will take the present at our hands' (1.1.118–20), he announces in mock-piety. As spectators, we see-saw turbulently between outrage at Richard's devilish duplicity towards his own brother and admiration at the superb performance he has just laid on.

One of the darkly hilarious moments in the play is the trap laid for Hastings. Originally an ally of Richard, Hastings is ruthlessly disposed of when his loyalty doesn't extend to betraying the lawful heir to the throne. But in order to eliminate as powerful a player as the Lord Chamberlain, Richard and his henchman, Buckingham, stage an elaborate playlet.

At a meeting of the Council, Buckingham first lulls the victim into a false sense of security. Flattering Hastings that he is the person present who is closest to the Duke of Gloucester, he elicits the complacent reply on Hastings' part that he knows the mind of the Duke. When Gloucester enters, Buckingham immediately passes on Hasting's presumptuous remarks, prompting Richard to assure the gathered company that 'Than my Lord Hastings no man might be bolder;/His lordship knows me well and loves me well' (3.4.31–2). The ostensibly generous words are oozing with dramatic irony—the spectators are privy to the plot of Richard and Buckingham to topple Hastings should he prove recalcitrant, although left in suspense as to how exactly it will play out.

Richard next move is a masterstroke of black humour. Turning to another member of the Council, the Bishop of Ely, he remarks, 'When I was last in Holborn,/I saw good strawberries in your garden there./I do beseech you, send for some of them' (36–9). The Bishop, eager to please, hastens to comply with the Duke's wishes. The humour emerges in the absurd juxtaposition of the mundane (strawberries) with the terrifying scenario that then unfolds.[16]

Richard has made a brief exit; when he returns, he pounces. He has changed from the affable, urbane conversationalist we saw at the beginning of the scene to a raving tyrant. He demands to know how to deal with those conspiring against his life. Holding up his crippled arm, he claims he has been cursed by witches, naming Hastings' mistress as one of the culprits. When Hastings hesitates in his response, Richard orders his execution for treason. What makes the scene so chilling is that it is common knowledge that Richard has been crippled from birth. Yet no one dares contradict him, and Hastings is sentenced to death.

Richard's strategy to gain power borrows heavily from Machiavelli's analysis of power politics in the *Prince*, in particular his advice to use both force and dissimulation, or to imitate the lion as well as the fox.[17] Machiavelli also lauds Cesare Borgia's use of shock and awe tactics. Always being a move ahead of others, and springing a surprise on them when they least expect it, is what he recommends to anyone who wants to retain power. The example Machiavelli gives is of the deputy Borgia sends in to restore order in the Romagna, which he has just conquered. His delegate, Remirro de Orco, cruel but efficient, does a good job but is greatly hated. One morning the citizens of Cesena wake up to find the hated deputy in two pieces in the square, with a block of wood and a sword by his side. 'This terrible spectacle left the people both satisfied and amazed' (26), Machiavelli remarks laconically. Machiavelli's account of Borgia's spectacle of violence is laced with more than a dash of grim humour. Similarly, the terrifying effect of Richard's own carefully staged performance of power is heightened by the banter about strawberries that comes immediately before the trap snaps shut.

What makes Richard, for all his monstrosity, so seductive is not only his infectious delight in his artistry, but his willingness to share his pleasure with the audience. His eagerness to talk to us gratifies our own vanity in being taken into the confidence of a character of such immense charm, intelligence—and ruthlessness. No doubt his appeal comprises the anarchic energy he exudes and his audacity in ignoring all moral norms, speaking to the secret fantasies to which most of us would never admit. But his allure is always tinged with menace. We laugh at his jokes because a part of us is relieved that we ourselves are not at the receiving end of his malicious humour.

The Netflix political thriller *House of Cards*, adapted from the 1990 BBC series and based on a novel by Michael Dobbs, derives largely from Shakespeare's *Richard III*. The British version traces the intrigues of a fictive Conservative Party Whip, Francis Urquhart, played with suave cynicism by Ian Richardson. The American adaptation charts the ascent to power by Congressman Frank Underwood and his wife Claire. Underwood, played by Kevin Spacey, is a modern-day Vice, who cultivates a special relationship with the audience while setting about the business of wresting power for himself.[18] He is also a masterly entertainer, winning our admiration for his canny persuasive skills and adroit manoeuvring, and his sharp insights into the pragmatics of power, which he delivers packaged as witty, cynical bon mots. Like Richard, he exudes a murderous charm, and by regularly breaking the fourth wall, lures the audience into the illusion that he has singled us out to share his confidences. Take, for instance, his monologue at the end of the first episode in the second season. Underwood has just murdered the journalist Zoe Barnes, with whom he has had an affair. It is not his first murder, and yet the moment in which he throws his former lover under a train at the metro station comes as a shock to viewers. At the end of the episode, we see Underwood in front of a dressing table, getting ready for dinner. Looking into the mirror, his eyes shift to gaze directly into the camera. 'Did you think I'd forgotten you?' he addresses the audience (Figure 4.2). And with just a touch of malice, he adds, 'Perhaps you'd hoped I had.' He then proceeds to elucidate why the murder was necessary.

> Don't waste a breath mourning Miss Barnes, every kitten grows up to be a cat. They seem so harmless at first—small, quiet, lapping up their saucer of milk. But once their claws get long enough, they draw blood, sometimes from the hand that feeds them. For those of us climbing to the top of the food chain, there can be no mercy. There is but one rule: hunt or be hunted.[19]

Figure 4.2 *House of Cards, Chapter 14* (2014), Dir. Carl Franklin, produced by MRC, Trigger Street Productions, Wade/Thomas Productions, Knight Takes King Productions

The blame, he explains, lies entirely on his lover for her lack of gratitude. He advises us to abandon every thought for her and to focus on the winners in society—like himself. Retaining the animal imagery, he expounds the social Darwinist theory of the survival of the fittest. But what is significant is the word 'us': he includes the audience in the circle of those heading for the top. Then he smiles. 'Welcome back', he says, with a glint of menace lurking under his bonhomie. We are welcome as long as we toe the line, applauding his cleverness and his jokes, he suggests. If not, we risk sharing the fate of Zoe Barnes. The vicious humour of the scene lies in the casual way Underwood discusses the murder of his lover, using the bizarre image of a kitten that has outgrown its use as a pet. The joke is underlined by the last shot of the camera, which zooms in on the cuff-links Underwood has been admiring. In a coded message that conveys his contempt for the audience, they bear his initials: FU.

Like *Richard III*, *House of Cards* is built on the basis of collaboration between audience and protagonist. Both Richard and

Frank Underwood manipulate the audience with a combination of flattery and fear. They operate in the secure knowledge that the audience is unreservedly behind them, approving their every move and cheering them on. Both works are a study in complicity. Underwood, now President of the United States, makes this explicit in a dramatic set piece that is initially addressed to the House Committee impeaching him for crimes ranging from obstruction of justice to abuse of power, but which segues into an address to the audience. In a stunning reversal, Underwood declares he is guilty. He then proceeds to turn the tables on his accusers. If he has been guilty of bribery or paying to play, he announces, in a wily metatheatrical pun, 'I accuse you of exactly the same', while the camera roams over the faces of the actors playing committee members. But the joke packs a more serious punch: all the politicians, he goes on to say, are in the pay of some master, or serving their own ambitions. If he is corrupt, so is the system, he claims. Extending the play on words, he argues, 'I am playing by the rules. The very rules you and I all agreed upon.' Underwood then turns directly to the audience.

> Oh, don't deny it. You've loved it. You don't actually need me
> to stand for anything, you just need me to stand. To be the
> strong man, the man of action. My God, you are addicted to
> action and slogans. It doesn't matter what I say. It doesn't
> matter what I do. Just as long as I'm doing something,
> you're happy to be along for the ride. And frankly, I don't
> blame you. With all the foolishness and indecision in your
> lives, why not a man like me? I don't apologize. In the end,
> I don't care whether you love me or you hate me, just as
> long as I win. The deck is stacked. The rules are rigged.
> Welcome to the death of the Age of Reason. There is no

right or wrong. Not anymore. There's only being in, and
then being out.[20]

If the President is destroying the ethical foundation of the
nation, Underwood asserts, the responsibility lies with us. For
wholly self-interested reasons, Underwood maintains, be it
the vicarious thrill of watching someone use strong-arm tactics to gain power in a way each of us can only dream of in
our sordid little lives, or out of sheer boredom, in our inces-
sant quest for sensation, we are happy to collude in his cynical
torpedoing of the system, and to accept his view of the political machinery as inherently fraudulent. The sociopath in the
White House is in effect our creation.

What Underwood forgets is the Machiavellian precept that
someone else, somewhere, is watching and learning. The new
breed of politician might be singularly lacking in charm and
irony, but they will be admired for the same ruthless instinct
for power as Underwood is, gratifying our own amoral crav-
ings. And however crude their tweets might be, they will use
a similar strategy of power, drawing us into complicity by
feeding our voracious hunger for sensationalism.

In one of his final moments in the Oval Office, Underwood lights a cigarette and then swiftly, before we've quite
realised what he is doing, burns a hole in the US flag at the
side of the presidential desk. Like the Joker, he doesn't quite
achieve his goal of burning everything down. This is because
he believes his orgy of destruction will be continued by his
successor, his wife, whose way to power he has paved. Once
she is in control, however, she betrays him, refusing to pro-
claim the presidential pardon he expects. The final joke is not
one Underwood makes but is a joke on him. It is also a joke
on us, his willing collaborators.

THE BANALITY OF EVIL

One of the more inane type of jokes circulating earlier this century (and currently experiencing a revival) is the 'knock-knock' joke, in which the set-up consists of a quick-fire series of questions and answers about who the person knocking on the door is, only to culminate in an atrocious pun. An early variety of the joke is to be found in *Macbeth*. In a climactic scene, Macbeth and his wife have just murdered Duncan, King of Scotland, who is staying under their roof. The murderous couple have committed regicide and violated the norms of hospitality into the bargain. While it is still dark, a knocking at the gate of Macbeth's castle is heard. Macbeth, seized by despair, gazes at his bloody hands as if they belonged to someone else and exclaims in horror: 'What hands are here? Ha, they pluck out mine eyes!' (2.2.62). Lady Macbeth takes command, firing off orders to her husband. Her solution is breathtakingly simple: 'A little water clears us of this deed' (70).

Next the porter emerges, rudely roused from his hangover. He grumbles that with a steady influx of visitors at all hours, the job is no better than being porter in hell. Spinning out the joke further, he runs through a list of potential callers at the gates of hell. These are a corrupt farmer, now a suicide, a traitorous equivocator, and a cheating tailor. Wearying of the jest, he announces, 'I'll devil-porter it no further' (2.3.14). When Macduff, Thane of Fife, enters, he begins a bantering exchange with the nobleman, spiked with sleazy jokes, ending with a mock-condemnation of alcohol for inducing impotence: 'Therefore much drink may be said to be an equivocator with lechery' (25–6). Then off he slouches.

We don't know how Shakespeare's contemporaries reacted to the scene, but in the centuries that followed, critics were appalled. The intrusion of low comedy into sublime tragedy was regarded as a transgression of the rules of decorum. Written a generation before *Macbeth* was first staged in 1606, Sir Philip Sidney's *Defence of Poesy* is a harbinger of neoclassical views, objecting to clowns thrust in 'by head and shoulders to play a part in majestical matters with neither decency nor discretion'.[21] With the inexorable rise of Shakespeare to cultural prominence, the idea was mooted, amongst others by Alexander Pope, that the scene hadn't been written by Shakespeare at all. Coleridge calls the scene 'disgusting', and declares, 'This low porter soliloquy I believe written for the mob by some other hand, perhaps with Shakespeare's consent . . . not one syllable has the ever-present being of Shakespeare.'[22] In performance, the scene was regularly cut, whether by William Davenant in his adaptation (complete with singing, dancing, and flying witches), or by David Garrick, who, despite vowing to revive the authentic Shakespeare, drew the line at the Porter.

Those who defended the scene saw it as a form of 'comic relief', drawing on an idea originally formulated by Dryden, who wrote, 'A Scene of mirth mix'd with Tragedy has the same effect upon us which our musick has betwixt the Acts, which we find a relief to us'.[23] De Quincey, the maverick Romantic critic, begged to differ. In a landmark essay, 'On the Knocking at the Gate in *Macbeth*' (1823), he argues that far from releasing the tension, the scene ratchets it up. The horror of the play is intensified by juxtaposing it with the Porter's tiresome ramblings. Since then, an army of critics has unearthed echoes of the main plot in the Porter's remarks. Equivocation is a theme that haunts the play, as is the gulf between aspiration and fulfilment. References to impotence and the disintegration of selfhood (as in the line by Macbeth cited above, recoiling from his own hands in horror) are frequent throughout the play. The sordid examples of greed, treachery, deceit, and desire the Porter mentions are a bathetic reflection of Macbeth's own character traits, serving to strip the tragic protagonist of any remnant of glamour.

The jesting porter is a secular version of the comic devil porters in mystery plays about the Harrowing of Hell, which represent Christ descending to the underworld to save the souls of the virtuous. Aptly enough, the Porter sees himself as a gatekeeper to the hellish castle of Inverness. But his jokes have a far more topical relevance. Historians have uncovered a wealth of allusions in the play to the Gunpower Plot of 1605, a Catholic conspiracy to overturn the government—equivocation was a technique advocated by Jesuit priests to allow Catholics, persecuted in Britain for decades, to remain truthful to God without incriminating themselves.[24] The Porter's jokes are aimed specifically at Father Henry Garnet, whose treatise in defence of the practice of equivocation was cited as evidence of his guilt for treason. 'Farmer' was a code name for Garnet, the remark about a tailor refers to a man who was said to have saved a relic from his martyrdom, while sneers about lechery reprise the salacious gossip about the Jesuit scholar.

The Porter is not merely mocking the murderous protagonist of the play. He is making a peculiarly nasty string of jokes about Jesuit priests, who, in a climate of anti-Catholic paranoia, were regularly hounded, tortured, and executed. This is the star turn in the Porter-jester's repertoire. What remain unclear is the work the jokes are doing. Is Shakespeare baiting Jesuits to play to the crowd? Or could it be the case that by making his jester a drunken lout, he is mocking the mockers, and the rabid anti-Jesuit propaganda that poured from the printing presses?[25]

Perhaps the thrust of the humour lies elsewhere. As it happens, Coleridge was right. The jokes are crude, the sentiments of the Porter coarse. The clumsy prose of the scene contrasts sharply with the lofty poetry in which the rest of the play is written. The Porter has none of the wit and perspicacity of killers like Richard III or Frank Underwood. Instead, the humour arises from the proximity between his drivel and the surrounding horror. The Porter is merely a small cogwheel in the machinery of terror, but happy to have a walk-on part. He reflects the savagery in which the play is steeped—and obliquely reflects the world in which the play is staged.

Before unlocking the gate, the Porter turns to the audience, like a Vice in a medieval play, reminding us to be generous in our tips: 'I pray you, remember the porter' (17). With its topical allusions and its direct audience address, the Porter scene briefly breaks the illusion of being set in medieval Scotland. It trains the spotlight on us. We laugh at the casual cruelty of the Porter not, as with charismatic bullies like Richard III or Frank Underwood, because we crave to be accepted in their circle. In the case of a vicious but despicable figure, we laugh with a mixture of contempt at his crassness and secret relief at not being the butt of his sadistic humour, happy to 'be along for the ride', as Underwood puts it. There is something distinctly uncomfortable about these moments of dark humour. Juxtaposing the terrifying with the trite not only intensifies the horror, as De Quincey claims, but also paradoxically works to trivialise that horror. This is the effect the text is aiming for—precisely in order to unsettle our complacent belief in our superiority to what is happening on stage. By taking pleasure in the absurdity of a degraded character, these moments suggest that we are in on the act, too.

Black humour that thrives on placing violence and banality side by side is a staple of contemporary culture. Film directors like Quentin Tarantino and the Coen Brothers have long demolished the conventional norms of good taste, exuberantly injecting humour into scenarios of brutality. One example is the black comedy crime drama *Fargo*, directed by Joel and Ethan Coen. Set in the ice-bound wastelands of North Dakota and Minneapolis, the plot turns on a car salesman, Jerry Lundegaard, who hires two small-time crooks to kidnap his wife for a ransom that Jerry hopes to extract from his rich father-in-law. The film is a withering comment on the petty greed and casual violence in which our world is saturated. The two hitmen are the epitome of stupidity and viciousness. They botch the job and leave a trail of clues for meticulous if plodding policewoman Marge Gunderson to follow. Played by Steve Buscemi and Peter Stormare as remarkably unattractive specimens of humanity, they consist of the voluble, manic Carl Showalter and his boorish, fish-eyed partner, Gaear Grimsrud, who continually quashes Showalter's clumsy attempts at small talk. A typical example is their dialogue on the car journey from Brainerd to Minneapolis. Carl gushes like a tourist guide, hoping to impress Grimsrud with his man-of-the-world act. Grimsrud remains impassive.

Carl:	Hey, look at that. Twin Cities. That's the IDS Building, the big glass one. Tallest skyscraper in the Midwest—after the uh, Sears, in, uh, Chicago, or John Hancock Building, whatever. You ever been to Minneapolis?
Grimsrud:	Nope.
Carl:	Would it kill you to say something?
Grimsrud:	I did.

At this point, Carl loses his patience. He switches to what he takes for a display of sarcastic wit.

Carl: 'No.' That's the first thing you've said in the last four hours. That's a, that's a fountain of conversation, man. That's a geyser. I mean, whoa, daddy, stand back, man. Shit. You know I'm sittin' here drivin', doin' all the drivin', man, the whole fuckin' way from Brainerd, drivin', just tryin' to chat, you know, keep our spirits up, fight the boredom of the road, and you can't say one fuckin' thing just in the way of conversation? Well, fuck it. I don't have to talk either, man. See how you like it. [*Pause*] Just total fuckin' silence. Two can play at that game, smart guy. We'll just see how you like it. Total silence.[26]

The problem is that Carl's stab at wit falls as woefully flat as his efforts at urbane conversation. His companion fixates him with a baleful gaze, unfazed by his threat of retreating into a sulk, while the audience chortle at the foolish figure he cuts. All the more jolting is the violence into which the film erupts during the next car ride, this time with the kidnap victim in the boot. Grimsrud embarks on an orgy of violence, killing a state trooper and two passers-by. Turning to the stunned Showalter, Grimsrud remarks contemptuously, 'You'll take care of it. You're a smooth smoothie, you know.' Grimsrud's taunt underscores his demonstration of being the more dangerous of the two, implicitly asserting his own claim to superiority. The menace he exudes is as sobering for the audience as for Showalter. Our laughter sticks in our throats.

HAMLET THE JIHADIST

Chris Morris' satire, Four Lions, follows a similar strategy to that of Fargo, using dark comedy to treat the theme of Islamic terrorism.[27] The film depicts a group of young British Muslims who dream of becoming suicide bombers. They are all dolt-ish amateurs: the imbecile, Faisal, the simple-minded but good-natured Waj, Barry, a British convert, an Islamic fanatic who is both vile and stupid, Hassan, a preening university-going rapper, and Omar, the sanest of the five, the only one who has a happy domestic life, with a loving wife and ador-ing son. Omar and Barry compete for the loyalty of the other members of the cell. They decide to blow up a target, but quarrel as to which is the most appropriate way to attack the society of 'kuffars' or infidels. Barry insists they need to bomb a mosque in order to 'radicalise the moderates', while Omar opposes his deranged plans. The group begin to build explo-sives and try them out in the countryside around Sheffield, where the film is set. Faisal, who has been instructing crows to act as carriers for bombs, tries out one of his trained birds, only to have it explode in front of him. Next, he trips in a field while carrying explosives and blows himself up. From now on, the presentation of the five stooges as harmless bunglers takes on a more sinister note and ends in their staging their jihadi stunt at the London marathon.

Where *Four Lions* differs from *Fargo* is by evoking sympathy for the clownish jihadists. It also has a number of interest-ing affinities with *Hamlet*. In many ways, Omar is presented as a tragic figure who is as confused as the dimwitted Waj, but who uses his persuasive skills to manipulate the others. A restless, alienated character, he is riven by doubts about the course they have chosen but is also eaten up by paranoia about the state and filled with revulsion at the consumerist culture in which we live. Tormented and narcissistic, he covets the role of leader of the group, allowing Barry's challenge to his power to influence his actions. All protagonists of the film, with the exception of Faisal, are obsessed with various forms of visual media, and spend hours posturing in front of the camera to make confession videos; the film is interspersed with films-within-films, and Omar is shown pouring over the outtakes of the films they have shot. His job is security guard at a shopping centre, surrounded by monitors. Omar projects himself as a hero, wreaking revenge on a corrupt world, a new version of Simba in the *The Lion King*—itself an adaptation of *Hamlet*—a story he tells his son at night. And both Hamlet and Omar brood upon death with a mixture of fear and fascination.

Much of the humour relies on slapstick and farcical gimmicks, such as the jihadists incessantly shaking their head in public to cause the surveillance camera photos to be blurred, or the fancy dress costumes they don for their heroic deed. The wittiest line is, however, delivered by Omar after he learns of Faisal's death, at which he was not present. Outraged, he demands, 'Where is he?' Hassan solemnly brings out a black bin liner. Barry immediately interpolates, 'It was a martyr's death', and attempts to glorify the accident: 'He disrupted the infrastructure . . . He took out a sheep . . . Attacked the food supply.' When Omar continues to glower, Hassan sheepishly confesses that bits of lamb are mixed up with Faisal in the bin liner. 'So what is he, is he a martyr or is he a fucking jalfrezi?', Omar explodes, metaphorically turning the remains of Faisal into a cannibalistic curry dish.

The savage joke is strangely resonant of a macabre jest cracked by Hamlet that plays on corpses, the food chain, and political subversion. After Hamlet has killed Polonius and is brought before the King, Claudius demands to know where the Prince has left the body.

King: Now, Hamlet, where's Polonius?
Hamlet: At supper.

King:	At supper? Where?
Hamlet:	Not where he eats, but where 'a is eaten: a certain convocation of politic worms are e'en at him. Your worm is your only emperor for diet. We fat all creatures else to fat us, and we fat ourselves for maggots. Your fat king and your lean beggar is but variable service, two dishes but to one table. That's the end.
King:	Alas, alas.
Hamlet:	A man may fish with the worm that hath ate of a king and eat of the fish that hat fed of that worm.
King:	What does thou mean by this?
Hamlet:	Nothing but to show you how a king may go a progress through the guts of a beggar.

(3.6.16–30)

Shakespeare's joke is far more sophisticated and multi-layered than is Omar's. It is also a classic example of Shakespeare's use of black humour. For a fleeting moment, Hamlet conjures up the surreal image of an assembly of worms at a feast, chomping away at the carcass of the King's counsellor. He then lectures Claudius about the status of worms in the food chain. Worms are at the very top of the sublunary chain of being and are thus superior to kings, he declares, at one stroke subverting the political order and upending the Elizabethan world picture. He elucidates this grotesque theory as follows: we eat animals, and worms eat us. For worms, it makes no difference whether the corpse they are feeding on is that of a king or that of a beggar. He elaborates the image further, reminding the King that worms are used as bait in fishing; these worms might have just had their fill of a royal cadaver. With a cannibalistic flourish, Hamlet points out that the fish caught with the bait of a worm that has fed off a king might end up on the plate of a commoner, or even someone at the bottom of the social hierarchy, like a beggar. What he is insinuating is that a king might end up being defecated from the bowels of a beggar.

The implicit *lèse-majesté* of these scatological remarks is of course intended to rile the King, and scandalises those attending him. The radical import of the joke is also intended as a coded political threat to Claudius, hinting at an overthrow of the ruling regime, and conveys a personal warning, playing incessantly, as the jest does, on dead kings. In addition, Hamlet manages to slip in a joke that slyly references the religious conflicts of the time. The puns on 'worm' and 'diet' gesture towards the Diet (or Council) of Worms held by Emperor Charles V in 1521 at which Martin Luther was summoned to defend his views. The question of transubstantiation was crucial to religious controversy between Catholics and Protestants and centred on the range of views about the Eucharist. According to the Church of Rome, the sacramental bread and wine were miraculously transformed into the body and blood of Christ, while from the most radical Reformed viewpoint, the Lord's Supper was only a symbolic act. Lavatorial jokes about what happened to the host after digestion by believers abounded in the polemical battle fought between the factions in cheap print.[28]

What tends to be overlooked in this dazzling blitz of wit is that Hamlet has just committed a murder. Although Hamlet cleverly manages to sidetrack the exchange to a discussion of the corpse of a king, the original corpse at issue is that of Polonius, whom Hamlet has stabbed to death while at his mother's closet. When Claudius insists, 'Where is Polonius?', Hamlet answers mockingly, 'In heaven' (31–2). In another dark wisecrack, Hamlet adds that those searching for him will soon be able to find him by following their noses—they will smell the putrefying corpse.

The idea of Hamlet as a jihadist is not new. In 1930, G. Wilson Knight drew attention to the self-righteous, zealous streak in Hamlet, and detected shades of Nietzschean hubris in him. Hamlet, he claims, increasingly displays signs of 'the nihilism of the superman'.[29] A recent adaptation of the play by Suleyman Al Bassam, an Anglo-Kuwaiti playwright, titled *The Al-Hamlet Summit*, portrays Hamlet as an Islamic extremist.[30] What Omar shares with the Prince is their refusal to take responsibility for their actions.[31] Instead, both Omar and Hamlet resort to black humour as a tactic to help them wrestle with their rage and despair at the injustices of the world—and to deflect attention from their guilt, perhaps even to themselves. Omar rants at his comrades, blaming them for Faisal's death, and refuses to face the fact that as the most intelligent member of the unit, he bears the burden of responsibility for not putting a stop to their lunacy long before Faisal was sacrificed. At the end of *Hamlet*, the Prince apologises to Polonius' son, Laertes, for the injustice he has done him (by now a second member of Polonius' family has fallen victim to Hamlet's actions, Laertes' sister Ophelia). But what begins as an apology soon veers into diverting the blame onto Hamlet's mental affliction. 'Was't Hamlet wronged Laertes? Never Hamlet', he exclaims, explaining, 'Hamlet does it not; Hamlet denies it./ Who does it then? His madness' (5.2.204; 207–8). At the end of the play, Hamlet has been responsible for the deaths of five people, although, despite his ruminations on death, he does not commit suicide. Omar kills no one but himself, but in reality, he is the mastermind behind the plans of the gang. In creating the characters, Chris Morris, who wrote the script together with Jesse Armstrong and Sam Bain, may well have been influenced by the profile of the suicide bombers responsible for the 7/7 London underground bombings in 2005, in which, in addition to the four suicide bombers, fifty-two people were killed and 700 were injured. After the attacks, it emerged that the leader, Mohammed Sidique Khan, who left a videotaped statement, was a happily married family man and devoted father. As the leader of the unit, Omar also bears responsibility for the death of Faisal and for wilfully confusing Waj to serve his own priorities.

In many ways, Shakespeare sets the paradigm for a variety of black humour that shapes much of contemporary culture. His predilection for putting the commonplace in collision with cruelty is echoed in the work of film directors such as Tarantino, the Coen Brothers, and Chris Morris, who delight in darkly comic humour, while his creation of a charismatic jester driven by an inexorable will to power has been formative for figures such as the Joker in the Batman comic series and films and the sophisticated political satire in Netflix's *House of Cards*. A peculiar characteristic of Shakespeare's black comedy is its reflexive quality. To my mind, the main target of the jokes are the spectators. This strand of humour implicitly interrogates the pleasure we take in the meshing of comedy and brutality. In the case of Vice-like figures like Richard III, the dark comedy exposes our eagerness to laugh about things we would normally condemn as we oscillate between being flattered at being taken on board as a confidante and relief at being let off the hook ourselves. As regards humour about vile but stupid protagonists, we laugh in derision at jokesters or buffoons we despise, snug in our superiority. And when the dark comedy relates to characters, however flawed, with whom we sympathise, we share their technique of resorting to savage humour to cope with pain and anger and the terror of death, and to stave off guilt.

As all the examples we have looked at suggest, dark humour uncovers our collusion in creating humour out of disturbing, often horrific situations. It holds up a mirror to our hankering after humour and entertainment, and our complacency about our role in shaping the world in which the protagonists, and we ourselves, live. Hamlet rails against the depravity of a society which he rejects, glorifying a mythical age of true ideals, only to endlessly procrastinate about implementing the very same ideals. The suicide bombers rage against the materialistic values of the West, but are fascinated by electronic equipment, computer games, theme parks, and bargains offered by fast food chains. The most intelligent member of the group, Omar, models himself on a figure in Walt Disney's *The Lion King* and dubs the group 'Four Lions', adopted from the nickname of the English national football team, 'The Three Lions', seemingly oblivious of his deep investment in the consumerism he so insistently denounces. Even while we chuckle at the absurd antics of the would-be jihadists, the black humour of the film draws attention to our own immersion in the entertainment culture we no doubt deplore.

In one scene Ahmed, the insufferably po-faced, fundamentalist, but entirely pacific brother of Omar, who disapproves of his Western lifestyle but also of his murderous plans, tells him, 'Joking is weakness.' At the end of the film, we see Ahmed being interrogated prior to what the film suggests is an operation of extraordinary rendition to Egypt, the extrajudicial practice of sending suspects to another country in order to circumvent the original country's rigorous regulations about torture and detention. In the 'war on terror', the UK was involved in a number of cases. Ahmed is set up as a laughing stock, but without the touch of pathos that the film evokes with regard to the other characters. But he too is collateral damage in Omar's self-absorbed quest to become a hero.

NOTES

1 *Julius Caesar*, dir. Gregory Doran (Royal Shakespeare Company, Stratford-upon-Avon, 2012).

2 The term 'black humour' (or *l'humeur noir*) for a comedic treatment of disturbing subjects (such as death, violence, or cruelty) was coined in 1939 by the French writer André Breton, to whom surrealism owes its theoretical framework. See his essay 'Lightning Rod' in the volume *Anthology of Black Humour*, ed. Bréton, transl. Mark Polizzotti (San Francisco: City Lights, 1997), xiii–xix. He pays tribute to Jonathan Swift as the founder of black comedy. Also see J. L. Styan, *The Dark Comedy: The Development of Modern Comic Tragedy* (Cambridge: Cambridge University Press, 1962); Matthew Winston, 'Humour noir and Black Humor', in *Veins of Humor*, ed. Harry Levin, Harvard English Series 2 (Cambridge, MA: Harvard University Press, 1972), 269–84; and Maurice Charney, *Comedy High and Low: An Introduction to the Experience of Comedy* (1978; New York: Peter Lang, 1987), 105–15.

3 'The Life of Julius Caesar', *Plutarch's Lives of Noble Grecians and Romanes*, 88; 'The Life of Marcus Brutus', *Plutarch's Lives of Noble Grecians and Romanes*, 105.

4 See R. W. Van Fossen, 'Introduction', in *Eastward Ho*, by George Chapman, Ben Jonson and John Marston, ed. Van Fossen, The Revels Plays (Manchester: Manchester University Press, 1979), 4–7. Van Fossen mentions the theory that the offensive passages were added in performance.

5 See James Shapiro, *1599: A Year in the Life of William Shakespeare* (London: Faber and Faber, 2005).

6 For illuminating discussions of Cinna the poet, see Frank Kermode, *Shakespeare's Language* (London: Penguin Books, 2000), 85–95, and Smith, *This is Shakespeare*, 145–60.

7 On black humour in Shakespeare, see John Kerrigan, 'Shakespeare and the Comic Strain', in *Revenge Tragedy: Aeschylus to Armageddon* (Oxford: Clarendon Press, 1996), 193–216, and David Ellis, 'Black Comedy in Shakespeare', *Essays in Criticism* 51.4 (2001): 385–403.

8   www.theguardian.com/global/2019/dec/29/horror-films-and-how-the-clowns-are-fighting-back

9   Sandra Billington, *A Social History of the Fool* (Brighton: The Harvester Press, 1984).

10 The authoritative work on the Vice remains Bernard Spivack's *Shakespeare and the Allegory of Evil: The History of a Metaphor in Relation to His Major Villains* (New York: Columbia University Press, 1958).

11 T. S. Eliot, *Selected Essays* (New York: Harcourt, 1960), 105–6.

12 Alan Moore, Brian Bolland, and John Higgins, *Batman: The Killing Joke* (London: Titan Books, 1988). I am indebted to Vincent Bernard for discussions about *Batman*.

13 *The Dark Knight*, dir. Christopher Nolan, perf. Christian Bale, Heath Ledger (Warner Bros. Pictures, 2008).

14 For two recent illuminating discussions of *Richard III*, see Marjorie Garber, 'Richard III: The Problem of Fact', in *Shakespeare and Modern Culture* (New York: Anchor Books, 2008), 108–23, and Stephan Greenblatt, *Tyrant: Shakespeare on Politics* (New York: Norton, 2018), 53–95.

15 See Garber, 'Richard III: The Problem of Fact', 112–13.

16 The strawberries are mentioned in Shakespeare's source, Thomas More's *History of King Richard III*, but Shakespeare compresses the time in the scene to create the jarring effect.

17 Machiavelli, *The Prince*, trans. Russell Price, ed. Quentin Skinner and Russell Price, Cambridge Texts in the History of Political Thought (Cambridge: Cambridge University Press, 2018), 61–62. All further references in parentheses.

18 See James R. Keller, 'The Vice in Vice President: *House of Cards* and the Morality Tradition', *Journal of Popular Film and Television* 43.3 (2015): 111–15.

19 *House of Cards*, created by Beau Willimon, perf. Kevin Spacey, Robin Wright (Netflix, 2013–18), Season 2, Episode 1.

20 *House of Cards*, Season 5, Episode 13.

21 Sir Philip Sidney, *An Apology for Poetry*, ed. Geoffrey Shepherd, revised by R. W. Maslen, 3rd ed. (Manchester: Manchester University Press), 2002), 112.

22 Samuel Taylor Coleridge, 'Marginalia on *Macbeth*', in *Shakespeare: Macbeth: A Casebook*, ed. John Wain (Basingstoke: Macmillan, 1968), 86; 84. For an overview of responses to the Porter scene see Kenneth Muir,

'Introduction', in *Macbeth*, The Arden Shakespeare (London: Thomson Learning, 2002), xxv–xxxii.

23 The defence of comic interludes was voiced by Neander, Dryden's mouthpiece in his dialogue 'Of Dramatic Poesy: An Essay' (1668). See John Dryden, *Selected Criticism*, ed. James Kinsley and George Parfitt (Oxford: Clarendon, 1970), 50.

24 On the Jesuit policy of equivocation, see Perez Zagorin, *Ways of Lying: Dissimulation, Persecution, and Conformity in Early Modern Europe* (Cambridge, MA: Harvard University Press, 1990); for a historical background on the persecution of Jesuits in England, see Garry Wills, *Witches and Jesuits: Shakespeare's Macbeth* (Oxford: Oxford University Press, 1996).

25 See Richard Wilson, *Secret Shakespeare: Studies in Theatre, Religion and Resistance* (Manchester: Manchester University Press, 2004), 188–207, who argues that in the play Shakespeare was attempting to diverge blame from Catholic aristocrats, and for the second view, see Robert S. Miola, 'Two Jesuit Shadows in Shakespeare: William Weston and Henry Garnet', in *Shakespeare and Religion: Early Modern and Postmodern Perspectives*, ed. Ken Jackson and Arthur F. Marotti (Notre Dame: University of Notre Dame Press, 2011), 25–45.

26 *Fargo*, dir. Joel and Ethan Coen, perf. Frances McDormand, William H. Macy Steve Buscemi, Peter Stormare (Gramercy Pictures, 1996).

27 *Four Lions*, dir. Chris Morris, perf. Riz Ahmed, Nigel Lindsay, Kayvan Novak, Arsher Ali, Adeel Akhtar (Film4 Productions, 2010).

28 See Catherine Gallagher and Stephen Greenblatt, 'The Mousetrap', in *Practicing New Historicism* (Chicago: University of Chicago Press, 2000), 136–62.

29 G. Wilson Knight, 'The Embassy of Death', in *The Wheel of Fire: Interpretations of Shakespearian Tragedy*, 4th ed. (1930; London: Methuen, 1954), 17–46; 40.

30 The play was first performed in English in 2002. In 2004 it was staged in London in Arabic with English surtitles. For an incisive discussion, see Peter J. Smith, '"Under Western Eyes": Sulayman Al-Bassam's *The Al-Hamlet Summit* in an Age of Terrorism', *Shakespeare Bulletin* 22.4 (2004): 65–77.

31 For a brilliant recent reading of *Hamlet*, see Rhodri Lewis, *Hamlet and the Vision of Darkness* (Princeton, NJ: Princeton University Press, 2017).

Five

'They do but jest, poison in jest. No offense i'th' world'

Hamlet 3.2.217–18

In the contemporary world, humour has become the focus of a culture war. In 2005, the Danish newspaper *Jyllands-Posten* published twelve cartoons depicting Muhammed, a move that triggered an uproar in Muslim communities and led to violence and deaths across the world. In 2012, the French satirical weekly *Charlie Hebdo* featured its own cartoons of Muhammed. Three years later, two gunmen forced their way into the headquarters of the magazine and shot twelve people. Admittedly, not all attacks on humour involve horrific violence. On a less lethal scale, the American comedian Kevin Hart, announced as host of the film Academy Awards in 2019, was attacked for homophobic jokes he had tweeted eight years previously, and, after apologising, withdrew. In the same year, an allegedly anti-Semitic cartoon of Benjamin Netanyahu, Prime Minister of Israel, in the *New York Times* provoked an outrage. The newspaper apologised and stopped publishing political cartoons altogether. The Russian-British comic Konstantin Kisin made headlines in connection with a fundraising comedy event in January 2019 at the School of Oriental and African Studies at the University of London. He was issued with a 'behavioural

DOI: 10.4324/9780429317507-6

agreement form' warning him about topics such as 'racism, sexism, classism, ageism, ableism, homophobia, biphobia, transphobia, xenophobia, Islamophobia, or anti-religion or anti-atheism'. The contract helpfully catalogues the breadth of subject matter treated in jokes. Kisin refused to sign and withdrew.[1]

The solemn itemising of taboo subjects is of course comedy gold, and Kisin mined it enthusiastically. Curiously, the list recalls a similar enumeration of immoral practices from an earlier age: 'effeminate mixt Dancing, Dicing, Stage-playes, lascivious Pictures, wanton Fashions, Face-painting, Health-drinking, Long haire, Love-lockes, Periwigs, womens curling, pouldring, and cutting of their haire, Bone-fires, New-yeares-gifts, May-games, amorous Pastoralls, lascivious effeminate Musicke, excessive laughter, luxuriously disorderly Christmas-keeping, Mummeries'. All these 'sinfull, wicked, unchristian pastimes', according to Puritan writer William Prynne, are indissolubly bound up with the theatre.[2] In his thousand-page tirade against plays, Prynne claims that they stem from the devil himself, or his agents. He lashes out at drama for corrupting the morals of both audience and actors, inciting lascivious and depraved behaviour and inspiring them to mock at religion. He trains his fire on stage humour too: 'all they learne from them is but some scurril jests . . . to deride, quip, scorne, scoffe, mocke and floute' (5I2r). By laughing, the audience demonstrate their complicity with the vicious sentiments presented in the plays.

Prynne's work was the culmination of a wave of antitheatrical polemic from the 1570s to 1642, when the theatres were closed.[3] The writers were not only Puritans, but included staunch critics of Puritans such as Stephen Gosson, and hack playwrights such as Anthony Munday and Gosson himself.[4] In their tracts, the same arguments are exhaustively rehearsed: plays enflame lust, encourage sinful conduct, and foster idolatry. The polemicists also deplore on-stage jesting, which they claim is intrinsically linked to folly and sexual debauchery. As Gosson puts it, 'Comedies so tickle our senses with a pleasanter vaine, that they make us lovers of laughter, and pleasure, without any meane'.[5] Attacks on the theatre are partly fuelled by a rejection of the conditions of the early modern entertainment industry, excoriated by the pamphleteers for catering to gratification, not edification—at the same time as they cannily exploit it for their own purposes, in particular the market for cheap print.[6]

We might snicker at the type of immorality antitheatrical zealots castigate, but in truth, a similar impulse underlies contemporary attacks on humour and early modern attacks on the theatre. Like antitheatrical polemicists, contemporary critics of ethically unacceptable humour claim that audience laughter constitutes an endorsement of the attitudes underpinning the jokes.[7] To find an offensive joke funny, you need to share the assumptions upon which the joke is constructed. In addition, the argument goes, pernicious humour reflects the attitude of the comedian. The critics argue that jokes disparaging certain groups (sexist or racist jokes, for instance) have a direct impact on society by perpetuating harmful stereotypes and reinforcing social prejudice. Both movements are attempts to gain control over discourse in the public sphere—and to redefine what it is acceptable to laugh about.

Where discussions of the ethics of humour diverge from debates about free expression is the claim that objectionable jokes are simply not funny. Instead, critics argue, these jokes inflict distress on members of the community that is the butt of the joke. As they point out, these jokes thrive on humiliation and pain.[8]

THEORIES OF HUMOUR

As a potted history of the theories of humour shows, the issues of humiliation and pain have always shadowed debates about humour. In many ways, contemporary theories about humour are a series of footnotes to Plato. Plato points out that our pleasure in laughter is inevitably entangled with malice. He calls for state censorship of satire—comic artists who mock others should be banned or fined. In the ideal state, laughter should be strictly controlled. Furthermore, watching a comedy would inspire one to act the buffoon in real life. Humour, he believes, implies a lack of self-restraint and enables our lower natures to gain control over our rational selves.[9]

Plato's views laid the foundation for what is termed the superiority theory of humour. According this theory, humour is always fuelled by gratification in the humiliation of others and in their misfortune. A classic example is our *Schadenfreude* at watching someone slip on a banana skin. Thomas Hobbes memorably spelt out the heady pleasure involved: 'laughter is nothing else but sudden glory arising from some sudden conception of some eminency in ourselves, by comparison with the infirmity of others, or with our own formerly'.[10] Nothing is funnier than watching other people stumble. A variation on the superiority theory was propounded by Henri Bergson, who alleges that comedy demands 'a momentary anaesthesia of the heart', a transitory moment in which sympathy with our fellow beings is suspended.[11]

For Sigmund Freud too, humour expresses socially harmful impulses such as aggression or forbidden sexual urges. These are usually repressed in the interests of civilised coexistence, but find a cathartic release in laughter, particularly in response to jokes that treat taboo topics.[12] The so-called relief theory, like the superiority theory, focuses on the joke teller and the auditor, but a competing, third theory, the incongruity theory, takes a different approach. Thinkers such as Immanuel Kant, Arthur Schopenhauer, and Søren Kierkegaard take a careful look at what triggers humour and conclude that anything that violates our expectations in an unthreatening manner strikes us as funny.[13] More recently, philosopher John Morreall has refined the incongruity theory, drawing attention to the cognitive double-take that the perception of incongruity involves—the pay-off for resolving an incongruity or deviation from a norm that momentarily attracts our attention is pleasure. The theory claims to be broader than the other two because it offers an explanation for phenomena such as our pleasure in wordplay.[14]

Shakespeare has left us no theoretical reflections about humour. In this, he is unlike Ben Jonson, who, in his commonplace book, *Timbers, or Discoveries*, approvingly jotted down the censorious words of the Dutch scholar, Heinsius, who labelled laughter as 'a kind of turpitude'. (Never mind that Jonson has written some of the most hilarious comedies in the English language.)[15] What Shakespeare offers us instead is a wealth of material about how humour works in theatrical practice. Each joke is a miniature performance embedded within the larger framework of the play. What emerges from his plays is that jesting is a mode of communication; more helpful than the three theoretical approaches is a close look at the interaction between joke-crackers, their counterparts, what they are joking about, and the way they engage with the audience. In each scenario, a different combination of factors is in play—decisive is what the jokes do and what effect they achieve. In joking relationships, such as that between Hal and Falstaff, or Valentine and Turio in *Two Gentlemen of Verona*, relations of power are negotiated, both among rivals and among friends. Humour is used as a weapon of attack or defence, but also as a means to knit a group together, as in *Romeo and Juliet*, *Much Ado About Nothing*, or *The Merry Wives of Windsor*. For both men and women, wit is an instrument to acquire social distinction, or a flirtation gambit—the romantic comedies teem with examples. Sparkling repartee is cultivated by the smart set in *The Merchant of Venice*, *Love's Labour's Lost*, and *Much Ado About Nothing*, enacting paradigms for spectators to emulate, while Cleopatra, Beatrice, and Rosalind are peerless exemplars of wit, deploying humour to send up male delusions of grandeur, their obsessions with cuckoldry, and their partiality for sugary romance. With a wry touch of self-mockery, they also jest to keep anxiety at bay, to stay 'on the windy side of care', as Beatrice puts it (*Much Ado*, 2.1.277–78). It is true that one of the functions of jests is to disseminate social norms, but in practice, what is discernible is that humour subverts assumptions as much as it perpetuates them, often with the very same joke.

Shakespeare's comic entertainers, tailored to the star comedians in his company, encompass a variety of clowns and fools, but generally fall into two categories. Characters like Costard, Lance, Bottom, Speed, and Lancelot Gobbo—rustics, simpletons, or wily servants—ape the antics of their betters, the high-born protagonists in main plot, or, for the audience, comment on the main themes of the play. Alternatively, wise fools like Touchstone, Feste, Lavatch, and Lear's Fool, professional jesters in great houses or at court, offer an ironic commentary on human folly. Modelled on Erasmus' Dame

Folly, the wise fools are a personification of paradox, mixing nonsensical foolery with wisdom, and holding up a mirror to the audience in the bargain. Wise fools deflate the pretensions of the elite and humble the powerful. At the same time, they provide Shakespeare with a vehicle that enables him to probe the question whether the didactic impulse of satire is undercut by its entertainment value. The relationship between humour and power is something he explores through the figure of the malevolent jester, based on the medieval Vice, in characters such as Richard III, Iago, or Edmund.

Shakespeare's sunny comedies often teeter on the edge of darkness, and Shakespeare has some dark fun turning comic plots into tragedies and tragedies into a joke. Claudio's puerile obsession with cuckoldry in *Much Ado About Nothing* takes on a pathological hue in *Othello*, and the fraternal quarrel in *As You Like It* turns murderous in *King Lear*, while the plot of *Romeo and Juliet* is burlesqued in the performance of 'Pyramus and Thisbe' in *A Midsummer Night's Dream*. Dark humour is an undercurrent that runs through most of Shakespeare's plays; jokes which get mileage out of pain and humiliation serve to evoke uneasy laughter on the part of the audience, implicitly laying bare our complicity in the reality the play represents.

HUMOUR AND PAIN

Possibly the play richest in ferocious humour is *King Lear*. In a particularly ghoulish scene midway through the play, Cornwall and Regan discover that Gloucester has been conspiring to help Lear behind their back, and have him bound and interrogated. Ironically, it is Gloucester himself who plants the idea in their head for their next move. Under the battery of their questions, Gloucester turns to Lear's daughter and bursts out, 'I would not see thy cruel nails/Pluck out his poor old eyes,

149 **Humour and ethics**

nor thy fierce sister/In his anointed flesh stick boarish fangs' (3.7.56–8). He launches into an impassioned attack on the sisters' inhuman treatment of their father, ending on the ominous note, 'But I shall see/The wingèd vengeance overtake such children' (65–6).

His words ignite the sadistic couple's sense of humour. Seizing on his drastic imagery, Cornwall literalises Gloucester's words. He plucks out one of his eyes, boasting, with a punning flourish: 'See't shall thou never' (67). Not to be outdone, his wife demonstrates her own sparkling wit. 'One side will mock another' (71), she quips in mock-concern, demanding that the second eye be torn out in an act of charity. A servant with a marked lack of humour interrupts the fun, spoiling the joke. After dispatching him, Cornwell returns to the jesting vein when he carries out his wife's suggestion, farcically addressing the eye itself: 'Out, vile jelly! Where is thy luster now?' (83–4). Even while her husband, stabbed by the servant, is dying, Regan delivers a final sally. Ordering the blinded Gloucester to be turned out of doors, she jibes, 'let him smell/His way to Dover' (94–5).

The barrage of dark jokes in the play continues unabated. One is a cruel practical joke. Disguised as Poor Tom, Edmund leads his father to the highest cliff at Dover. Gloucester hopes to end his misery by flinging himself off the cliff. Edgar tricks the blind man into believing they are toiling up a steep path, and gives him a graphic description of the scene from the vertiginous heights he claims they have achieved—birds appear the size of beetles and 'fishermen that walked upon the beach/Appear like mice' (4.5.18–9). Gloucester makes a leap—and takes a pratfall. Although Edgar claims his ruse was intended to cure his father of his despair, what the audience sees is a callous joke played on a blind man.

In Shakespeare's most savage act of sabotage with regard to his sources, Edgar's remorse comes too late to save Cordelia. In a final harsh joke, Shakespeare cocks a snook at classical theories of drama, subverting the *anagnorisis*, the crucial moment in which the protagonist gains insight into the truth, by having Lear die ensnared in the delusion that Cordelia lives.[16] The grim humour of the play is summed up in Gloucester's words, 'As flies to wanton boys are we to th' gods:/They kill us for their sport' (4.1.38–9). Life is a huge joke, but those enjoying the fun are not the humans.

King Lear has been seen as encapsulating existentialist *Angst*, notably by the critic Jan Kott, who reads the play as a precursor of Samuel Beckett's *Endgame*.[17] The play's jokes about pain, loss, and horror underline the absurdity of the universe and the meaninglessness of human existence, he argues. In the light of human futility, our aspirations and despair are hilarious. Or as Nell in *Endgame* puts it, 'Nothing is funnier than unhappiness.'[18] In the words of Nietzsche, the philosopher who was an inspiration for existentialist thought, the reason why 'man is the only animal that laughs' is that 'he alone suffers so excruciatingly that he was compelled to invent laughter'.[19] Without pain, we wouldn't have laughter. In *Endgame*, humour is inextricably fused with pain. To face a world of grotesque brutality and endless misery, Beckett suggests, all we have is humour.

The conjunction of anguish, anger, and comedy in *King Lear* finds an uncanny echo in the stand-up comedy performed by the Australian comic Hannah Gadsby (Figure 5.1). Gadsby's show *Nanette*, first staged in 2017, sparked a media sensation for its shocking violation of generic norms—in particular by Gadsby's announcement, in the middle of the show, that she would quit comedy.[20] The show is organised around the

Figure 5.1 *Hannah Gadsby: Nanette* (2018), Dir. Madeleine Parry, Jon Olb, produced by Guesswork Television

theme of homosexuality and humour, and is remarkable for its searing jokes and its probing meditation on the art of comedy. Gadsby draws on her own history as a lesbian growing up in Tasmania in the 1990s, where homosexuality was a crime until 1997 and which she had to leave as soon as she found out she was 'a little bit lesbian'. She narrates a funny story about how she was almost beaten up by someone who thought she was a man flirting with his girlfriend, only to discover at a closer look that she was a woman and thus out of bounds. Self-disparaging humour is Gadsby's forte. Even her gayness doesn't hold up to scrutiny: describing how a censorious lesbian spokeswoman ('self-appointed', as Gadsby is quick to add) approached her after a show complaining that there was 'not enough lesbian content', Gadsby makes a crest-fallen confession. 'I don't think I'm very good at gay', she observes apologetically, adding, 'I should quit, I'm a disgrace.' The butt of her joke is the identity police, at whom she takes another dig when she relates how another spectator declared that she had an obligation to identify as transgender. Bemused, Gadsby comments that what she really identifies as is tired.

Then she swivels around to rip apart her trademark humour—and comedy itself. Self-deprecation, she reflects, is not humility: 'it's humiliation'. As she explains, 'I put myself down in order to speak, in order to seek permission to speak.' As a gay comedian, she is abasing herself in order to elicit laughter, she notes, and declares she is no longer willing to do so. Her career as comedian is over, she announces. The show proceeds to reveal dizzying depths of pain and rage in Gadsby, hollowed out by traumatic events in her past. In a brilliant move, she returns to the funny story she began her performance with and reveals that by turning the anecdote into a joke, she has been complicit in a lie. For in reality, the man returned, recognising her as a lesbian. She was beaten to pulp and too consumed by self-hate to go to hospital or to the police. She also fleetingly touches on the sexual abuse and rape that she has experienced. 'I need to tell my story properly', Gadsby asserts. In a meticulous anatomy of how humour works, she points out that the building blocks of jokes are tension and release. Jokes exploit trauma for a punch line. What is required for a healing to take place is narrative, which ends in closure. 'Laughter is not our medicine. Laughter is just the honey that sweetens the bitter medicine. Stories hold our cure', Gadsby wraps up, leaving the audience stunned at the rawness of the emotions that she has uncovered.

Nanette is a reminder of how closely humour is enmeshed with pain and humiliation. It is also striking that in some respects, Gadsby has affinities with antitheatrical campaigners, making a powerful case against a global comedy industry that peddles pleasure and cathartic release from tension.

Driven by the urge to expose sexual violence, homophobia, and misogyny, she is only too aware of the dangers of humour: enabling her audience to evade responsibility for social injustice. Her programme enacts a paradox: one of the most sophisticated comedy shows to emerge recently categorically repudiates humour. Ironically, however, it is precisely Gadsby's use of the comic medium that enables her to take control of her pain and transmit her story to a wide audience. As a consummate comedian, she wields enormous power over her audience, using laughter to fuse them into a community. She winds up her programme with an appeal for 'the story we need: connection'. But as she herself demonstrates, this is one of the functions that humour can fulfil.

Gadsby's wrenching farewell to comedy is in fact an intrinsic part of her performance. No one is funnier about unhappiness than Gadsby. What the show demonstrates is how humour is both an instrument of humiliation and a technique of resistance, a tool to inflict violence and a tactic to cope with pain. Humour might not be the best medicine (penicillin is better, Gadsby notes drily), but as both Shakespeare and Gadsby, despite her rejection of comedy, imply, it is a survival strategy in a world of terror and desolation, providing a source of resilience and an antidote to pain.[21]

As it happens, Gadsby did not quit comedy. A year later, she toured the comedy circuit with another show, *Douglas*, in which she delivered a dazzling new variation on the themes of pain, identity, and art.

A JOKE TOO FAR

One way the theatre responded to antitheatricalist attacks was by absorbing some of its premises.[22] But it also retaliated against the Puritans by turning them into a joke. The stage puritan was a fabrication that caricatured Protestant zealots as the epitome of hypocrisy, their devoutness a veneer for greed or lechery.[23] Shakespeare's contribution to this stock character, Malvolio in *Twelfth Night*, is, however, a more subtle creation. When he intrudes upon the fun the assorted spongers, retainers, and hangers-on at Olivia's house are having and chastises them for their behaviour, they decided to take revenge on him. A discussion ensues about Malvolio's identity. Maria observes that 'sometimes he is a kind of puritan', at which the fatuous Sir Andrew exclaims, 'Oh if I thought that, I'd beat him like a dog.' When Sir Toby demands the reason for his assertion, Sir Andrew flounders: 'I have no exquisite reason for't, but I have reason good enough.' Maria clinches the debate by retracting the remark she has just made, instead attacking Malvolio for being a toady: 'The devil a puritan that he is, or anything constantly but a time-pleaser, an affectioned ass' (2.3.129–36).

The play puts forward the suggestion that Malvolio's unpleasant traits are due to his religious beliefs—only to immediately undermine the idea. There is little sense of piety about Malvolio, who never speaks in a godly idiom and who, during the absurd catechism by Feste as Sir Topas later in the play, expresses religious views that are wholly orthodox. What we observe is a petty figure of authority consumed with self-importance. Maria confirms this view: 'The best persuaded of himself—so crammed, as he thinks, with excellencies—that it is his grounds of faith that all that look on him love him' (137–40). It is not moral zeal that animates Malvolio, but a vastly inflated opinion of himself.

His opponents are impelled by a rag-bag of motives. As a knight and kinsman of Olivia's, Sir Toby chafes at being disciplined by his social inferior. 'Art any more than a steward?', he sneers. He also resents the sanctimonious attitude that Malvolio strikes. 'Dost thou think because thou art virtuous, there shall be no more cake and ale?', he demands (105–7). His lines resonate with the larger historical backdrop of the culture wars in the early modern period. The sweeping campaign by Reformers to purge popular culture of the vestiges of paganism led to a rigorous curtailing of ritual festivity and a ban on religious drama, May games, and church ales, while all forms of celebration were regarded as a threat to order and morality. It is this Lenten impulse that Malvolio seems to embody.

For Maria, a fellow attendant at the household of Olivia, Malvolio is a rival vying for the trust of their mistress, as his threat to report her to Olivia reveals. Significantly, Maria's plan is to make him lose face in the eyes of Olivia. She unerringly identifies the main impulse that drives Malvolio: social aspiration. Accordingly, the forged letter dangles the promise of social climbing through marriage in front of him by reminding him that 'some have greatness thrust upon 'em' (2.5.127–8). All he need do is grasp the opportunity bestowed on him.

For Feste, professional self-respect is at stake. Earlier in the play, we see Malvolio disparage his jesting to his patron, Olivia, jeering at him as 'a barren rascal' (1.5.75–6) who has run out of jokes. Fabian and Andrew, in the meantime, are driven by a vague animus against Malvolio's puritanical traits. Fabian complains that Malvolio informed on him to Olivia in connection with a bear-baiting that he once organised—Puritans were vocal in their hostility to blood sports—while Sir Andrew flails out at Brownists, a radical sect of Puritans: 'I had as lief be a Brownist as a politician' (3.2.26–7). Once again, the play suggests that at least some of his enemies are keen to label Malvolio a Puritan.

Framed as a miniature play-within-a-play, the gulling scene reveals the workings of humour by punctuating the actions of Malvolio with the running commentary produced by his eavesdroppers. The effect is to ratchet up the hilarity of the scene: as in a hall of mirrors, the laughter of the on-stage spectators and the laughter of the audience ricochet off each other. In addition, the remarks by the on-stage spectators contain comic nuggets: Sir Andrew, for instance, absurdly flattered at being singled out by Malvolio in his rambling monologue, blithely ignores the fact that he has been dubbed 'a foolish knight' (2.5.69). The jest capitalises on Malvolio's boundless conceit, showing how he swallows the bait of the bogus letter with its preposterous instructions without a moment of hesitation. After Malvolio appears in carnivalesque garb to Olivia, as instructed in the letter, and makes a thorough fool of himself, the jest-crackers taunt him in a burlesque of Puritan rhetoric, pretending to believe he has been possessed by the devil and marvelling at 'how hollow the fiend speaks within him' (3.4.85). Over the centuries, the glorious joke has triggered gales of audience laughter. Shakespeare permits himself a brief self-congratulatory moment when he has Fabian boast, 'If this were played upon a stage now, I could condemn it as an improbable fiction' (115–16).

It is at this point that mood of the scene sours. The conspirators are unable to resist the chance to push the joke further. Maria urges that they pursue their victim, and Sir Toby suggests that they have him bound and confined in a dark room, a customary treatment for the insane. Only Fabian raises a doubt. 'Why, we shall make him mad indeed', he warns his fellow plotters, to which Maria answers grimly, 'The house will be the quieter' (120–21). The second instalment of the joke consists of Feste playing a curate, Sir Topas, and tormenting the imprisoned Malvolio by pretending to believe he has lost his wits. Although it contains a clever comic set piece, Feste's dialogue in alternating voices as Sir Topas and himself, the humour remains flat. In contrast to the gulling scene in the garden, Malvolio's lucid words stand in stark contrast to the garbled nonsense of the clown, who attempts to trip him up with doctrinal gibberish. The sense that the joke is no longer funny is underlined by Sir Toby, who now regrets carrying the jest further than planned. 'I would we were well rid of this knavery' (4.2.63), he complains, fearing the disapproval of Olivia.

In the gulling of Malvolio, Shakespeare explores a question that consumes contemporary cultural discourse: when does a joke go too far? The play is tantalisingly equivocal about whether or not Malvolio is a Puritan. This is quite different in the case of other stage puritans. Jonson's creations—Zeal-of-the-Land Busy in *Bartholomew Fair*, or the Anabaptists Tribulation and Ananias in *The Alchemist*—are grotesque caricatures whose pious drivel is a cloak for gluttony, lust, avarice, and sedition, traits conspicuous by their absence in Malvolio. (Even his name is more evocative of Italianate comedy than of real-life Puritans). Most Puritans disapproved of jesting as a sign of frivolity, and frowned upon scoffing at others, but these views were shared by divines across the entire spectrum of religious denominations, from Jesuits to Brownists.[24] What is clear is that in *Twelfth Night*, Malvolio's opponents, for a variety of reasons, have a stake in framing him as a religious zealot. They implicitly compare their joke to the sport of bear-baiting. In revenge for Malvolio's thwarting their fun, Sir Toby promises Fabian that 'To anger him we'll have the bear again, and we will fool him black and blue' (2.5.8–9).

By showcasing the role of spectatorship in a jest, both on stage and in the auditorium, Shakespeare draws attention to the contribution of the audience in the generation of humour. As he demonstrates, a joke requires audience collaboration; humour is something a community of laughers create through laughter, in collusion with the joke teller. We choose to find something funny. Contemporary custodians of humour are right: taking pleasure in a joke signals willingness, at least momentarily, to entertain the ideas it is built around.

Nor is our society the first to aim to discipline humour, although the yardstick applied varies considerably. On the one hand, in *De Oratore* Cicero has his speaker Gaius Julius Caesar Strabo, known for his wit, enthusiastically recommend ugliness and bodily defects as topics for jokes, although he warns his listeners to avoid excessive, buffoonish humour and facial distortion (2.239). The early modern rhetorician, Thomas Wilson, is even more explicit. 'Sometimes we jest at a man's body that is not well proportioned, and laugh at his countenance if either it be not comely by nature or else he, through folly, cannot well see it', he announces. There is no need to distinguish carefully between congenital defects and foolish vanity, he implies, since outer deformity is a reflection of inner flaws.[25] On the other hand, Thomas More, an equally avid collector of jokes, writes that in Utopia, 'To mock a person for being deformed or crippled is considered disgraceful, not to the victim, but to the mocker, who stupidly reproaches the cripple for something he cannot help.'[26] And in his discussion of ideal dinner-table conversation, Plutarch stresses the importance of tactful jesting. The art of conversation consists of 'the knowledge and observance of good taste in question-posing and fun-making', he declares.[27]

If finding something funny is a choice, the corollary is that humour can be cultivated. For Aristotle, moral virtues (amongst which he includes wittiness) are acquired through repeated acts, and over time, become habitual. As he points out, we are not born with innate virtues—'we become just by doing just acts, temperate by doing temperate acts, brave by doing brave acts'.[28] The same applies to pleasures and pains. We can train ourselves in what we take pleasure.

BEING OFFENDED IS A CHOICE

At the end of *Twelfth Night*, a letter written by Malvolio is delivered to Olivia. Quite in character for Malvolio, the letter articulates a mixture of resentment and threat. After Fabian gives the company an account of the 'sportful malice' (5.1.353) and delivers a plea that, considering that both sides bear responsibility for the events, the quarrel be dissolved in laughter, Olivia turns to Malvolio to express her sympathy. Malvolio refuses to accept it. Reprising the imagery of bear-baiting, he threatens the company: 'I'll be revenged on the whole pack of you' (364).

The last of Shakespeare's festive comedies, *Twelfth Night* is not the only comedy to end on a discordant note. *Love's Labour's Lost* ends with a parting of ways between the ladies and the lords; in *The Merchant of Venice*, Shylock slinks out of the courtroom and the play; in *Much Ado About Nothing*, after his crimes are uncovered, Don John flees; and in *As You Like It*, Jaques prefers exile to joining the celebrations. *Twelfth Night* leaves a trail of loneliness and melancholy in its wake.[29] But it is also the only comedy to abandon a semblance of reconciliation for one of the decisive conflicts in the play, breaking off on a note of fury and outrage.

Twelfth Night does not only grapple with the limits of humour. It also raises the question whether the same sense of decorum might apply in the case of being offended. Taking offence, the play suggests, is a choice, too. We are responsible for how we respond to humour. In his self-righteousness and sense of grievance, Malvolio is a role model for our own age. Contemporary comedy often bears the brunt of our increasing sensitivities. Ricky Gervais, who argues that comedy is by nature provocative and specialises in abrasive jokes, points out that in an age of Internet and social media, when jokes are lifted out of their performative context, inevitably someone, somewhere, will find a joke objectionable. Emphatically rejecting the moral high ground taken by those who consider themselves the victims of disrespect, he claims, 'Just because you're offended doesn't mean you're right.'[30]

Our readiness to take jokes personally is not just a symptom of our tender self-regard, but is also rooted in our narrow definition of identity and our insistence on identifying solely with self-contained communities. By evading a clear designation of Malvolio as a Puritan, Shakespeare challenges the idea that we reject or identify with someone on the basis of their membership in a specific group. Contrary to general belief, a number of Puritans frequented the theatre, as Prynne admits (V4v), and many playwrights harboured Puritan sympathies.[31] Would they have identified with Malvolio by dint of belonging to the same denomination? Or would they rather have regarded their identity as consisting of a multiplicity of facets, only few of which they shared with as insufferable a prig as Malvolio? In the case of jokes about specific groups, the issue is further complicated by the radical ambiguity inherent in humour. Jokes about ethnic groups such as Jews or Blacks can acquire an entirely different meaning depending on the context in which they are uttered. An anti-Semitic joke might be relished by a racist audience; the very same joke might be pressed into service by Jews to mock the anti-Semitic stereotypes circulating among non-Jews. Or

Humour and ethics

161

to mock *other* type of Jews from which the joke teller and their audience would wish to distance themselves.

In Shakespeare's own time, a thinker whose ideas experienced a surge of popularity was Seneca. In response to a world shattered by religious and political turmoil, late sixteenth-century Europe saw a revival of Stoic thought. Today, Stoicism is usually associated with dour moralists. Less well-known are Seneca's comments on offensive jokes. In his essay 'On Constancy', Seneca points out that those who are easily insulted are pampered natures who have too much leisure to cultivate their sense of injury. In order to pull the rug from under the feet of those who jeer at you, he recommends an entirely different strategy: self-mockery. 'No one becomes a laughing-stock who laughs at himself', he argues.[32] Citing the example of Socrates, who laughed at the jokes about himself in Aristophanes' *Clouds*, Seneca insists that depriving one's enemies of the pleasure of offending one is a form of revenge.

A recent example that does Seneca proud is the response of the Kazakhstan tourism board to Sacha Baron Cohen's film, *Borat Subsequent Moviefilm*, released in 2020. The first Borat film in 2006 met with official fury for its depiction of Kazakhstan as a benighted nation and was promptly banned. In our age of outrage and cancel culture, the second film ignited a storm on social media. Predictably, the Kazakh American Association accused the film of promoting 'racism, cultural appropriation and xenophobia', ticking all available boxes, however oxymoronic. An online petition demanded that the film be cancelled for humiliating Kazakhstan and 'the dignity of the Kazakh nation'. By contrast, the tourism board chose a different strategy. It adopted an ingenious suggestion mooted by an American and Kazakh duo, who filmed a number of advertisements to promote tourism in Kazakhstan using Borat's catchphrase,

'Very nice!' The clips show tourists hiking, armed with a selfie stick, tucking into traditional food, admiring the technological wonders of the country, and posing for photographs with the natives. Throughout, they lavish praise on everything Kazakh as 'Very nice!' The advertising campaign nicely combines a dig at Sacha Baron Cohen with gentle mockery of tourists as reverse Borats and canny marketing, capitalising on the Borat phenomenon while skimping on the fees due to the inventor of a slogan. In its own cultural appropriation of Baron Cohen's ideas, it deploys humour as a weapon in a subtle form of revenge.[33]

TALKING SHIT IS AN ART

One of the most brilliant contemporary comedians, Dave Chappelle, revels in shock humour (Figure 5.2). In his 2019 comedy show, *Sticks & Stones*, he tackled the furore caused by a documentary that was aired earlier that year, *Leaving Neverland*, which provided graphic details of the allegations of sexual abuse brought forward against Michael Jackson by two victims. 'I'm gonna say something that I'm not allowed to say', Chappelle begins, priming his audience for the provocation. He begins by flatly denying the allegations. Then he doubles back. Pretending to reconsider, he comes up with an outrageous argument. 'Even if he did do it . . . I mean, it's Michael Jackson', he points out with a mischievous grin, insinuating that the victims should feel honoured. Conceding that 'more than half the people in this room have been molested in their lives', he persists: 'But it wasn't no goddam Michael Jackson, was it?' He continues to hone the joke, recounting a fantasy conversation among boys at school the next day about how they spent the weekend. Among his peers, the boy who can claim he was molested by the King of Pop would have hit the

Figure 5.2 *Dave Chappelle: Sticks & Stones* (2019), Dir. Stan Lathan, produced by Pilot Boy Productions

jackpot. To add insult to injury, Chappelle winds up, 'I know it seems harsh, but, man, somebody's gotta teach these kids. There's no such thing as a free trip to Hawaii.'[34]

As Chappelle no doubt intended, the joke set off a howl of righteous anger. Chappelle was accused of blaming the victim rather than condemning the perpetrator and of condoning sexual abuse. The detractors fell into the trap that Chappelle had laid. The critical response confirms the larger point Chappelle is making about our hunger for sensationalism in any form, and our prurient fascination with the private lives of celebrities. Chappelle is in fact addressing a range of serious issues—the distinction between art and artist, the sanctified status accorded to presumed victims, and our pleasure in killing the thing we love—but more importantly, his jokes enact precisely the skewed priorities in cultural and political debate that he is lambasting. At the heart of the show is an abuse that

Chappelle has repeatedly targeted: America's disastrous lack of gun control. In a tongue-in-cheek routine that rips racial stereotypes about violence to shreds, he muses, 'I don't see any peaceful way to disarm America's whites.' There is only one thing that is going to save America, he declares. Turning to address Black members of the audience, he urges them to fulfil their patriotic duty: 'Every able-bodied African-American must register for a legal firearm.' This, he implies, would immediately generate stricter gun laws.

Sometimes, as Chappelle shows, jokes are not really about their ostensible subject matter, but about something else entirely. In the routine about Michael Jackson, Chappelle slips into the persona of someone who harbours sympathy for paedophilia and urges the victims of Michael Jackson to show gratitude for having been selected for abuse by the legendary artist. Chappelle is playing games with the predilection of culture warriors to identify a performance with the performer and to take the words of a joke at face value. But stand-up comedy is a dramatic art which obeys the same rules as every other fictive presentation. In other words, it is a performance. And jokes are fictions, shaped by generic conventions, which include features such as exaggeration and distortion. A trait proponents of cancel culture share with antitheatricalists is the propensity to collapse the boundaries between fiction and truth. Inspired by the programmatic goal of Reformers to free Scripture from the accretions of convention and return to the true Word of God, attacks on the theatre were marked by a rigid literalism, assuming that the surface meaning of a fiction corresponded to its actual meaning. For antitheatricalists, taking pleasure in fictions about reprehensible acts was equivalent to approving of these acts. As Prynne states categorically, spectators who enjoy scenes of wantonness and on-stage jesting 'delight not in the representations onely of sinne, but even in sinne it self' (6E4r). What both contemporary humour vigilantes and Puritans ignore is that cultivating ambivalence or layers of meaning is a characteristic feature of aesthetic artefacts. Few imaginative products are more decisively defined by ambiguity than jokes. In contrast to everyday language, for instance, where ambiguity is a source of misunderstanding, in humour ambiguity is a source of pleasure.

Some theorists argue that humour is best understood as a form of play, a separate realm which, like art, belongs in the sphere of the imagination. The classic definition of play by Johan Huizinga still holds: it is 'a free activity standing quite consciously outside "ordinary" life as being "non serious"'. Furthermore, it 'proceeds within its own proper boundaries of time and space according to fixed rules'.[35] Humour theorists argue that humorous discourse is a special type of language for which the rules are different from those that apply in serious communication. As Michael Mulkay explains, 'In the humorous domain the rules of logic, the expectations of common sense, the laws of science and the demands of propriety are all potentially in abeyance.'[36] Engaging with a joke means temporarily being willing to enter into an imaginative arena governed by the laws of make-believe. As with drama, this involves being aware simultaneously of two frames of reference, that of the non-serious world and that of the real world.[37] Wittgenstein compares sharing a joke to playing a ball game. Those willing to play the game catch the ball and throw it back; 'but certain people might not throw it back, but put it in their pocket instead', signalling their refusal to join the game.[38]

Juggling two different worlds, the play world with the real world, was something at which Shakespeare excelled. The early modern term 'jest' does not refer merely to an exploit or a prank, but could also refer to a performance, like a pageant or a masquerade. It includes the connotations of make-believe, a world of 'as-if', as in the expression 'in jest'.[39] In a response to the literalism of the antitheatricalists, the theatre developed a sophisticated technique of self-reflexive debate, exploring the reverberations of its own artifice in metadramatic moments. Usually discussed as a serious, quasi-Brechtian reflection on the dangers of illusion, Shakespeare's metadrama can also be very funny. 'Metajokes' are jokes that make jokes about jokes, playing with generic conventions, for instance, by deliberately refusing to deliver a punchline ('Why did the chicken cross the road? To get to the other side.')[40] Shakespeare's metatheatrical moments foreground the mechanics of theatrical fiction—which, in many ways, mirror the mechanics of humour. Like metajokes, these self-conscious vignettes remind us that fictions are a pleasurable suspension of everyday life and offer an incursion into an illusory world. For an evanescent moment, metadramatic moments also jolt us out of our ceaseless self-absorption, enabling us to take a step back and see things from a distanced perspective.

Falstaff, Shakespeare's most towering comic creation, is the quintessence of play.[41] He dominates the plays he is in, but also always draws attention to his status as star entertainer. Straddling the world of the playhouse and the fictive world, he plays to his audience in both realms, exemplifying the principle that humour is always a mutual game between audience and performer. As paradigmatic player, whose zest for play is infectious, he embodies the notion of jesting as a pastime pursued above all for pleasure. He revels in slipping into an imaginative world with each outrageous jest: redefining his criminal activities as labouring 'in his vocation' (1.2.92), himself as 'a valiant lion' (2.4.250), and lecturing the Lord Chief Justice (a man of his age), 'You that are old consider not the capacities of us that are young' (2HIV 1.2.159–60). What he also personifies is the notion that identity consists of a profusion of selves jostling each other within us and changing all the time. A metadramatic moment that highlights the layered implications of Falstaff's role-playing for the practice of jesting is the play-within-a-play in Henry IV Part 1.

Falstaff's lies about the Gadshill incident have just been exposed in front of the Eastcheap crew by Hal. To prevent a further loss of face, Falstaff immediately suggests, 'Shall we have a play extempore?' (2.4.254–5). Accordingly, Falstaff and Hal stage a double act in which they play out an imaginary conversation between the King and Hal, armed with props like a cushion, a joint stool, and a dagger (to represent a crown, a throne, and a sceptre, respectively). The playlet demonstrates Falstaff's ease in slipping into roles, delighting his on-stage audience as much as the spectators of the play. His parody of the King has, however, the additional effect of destabilising the very notion of essential kingship. His mocking question, 'Shall the son of England prove a thief and take purses?' (373) will resonate through the play, as we increasingly note that the actions of the ruling class are merely a variation on the petty crimes of the low-life characters. And Hal will emerge as no less a role-player than Falstaff, though he plays with higher stakes. When in the play-within-a-play Hal takes over the role of his father and launches an attack on his former mentor as an 'abominable misleader of youth' (421), Falstaff pleads in his own defence. Expelling him would be akin to denying life itself: 'Banish plump Jack and banish all the world' (437). He is large; he contains multitudes, he reminds us, articulating a concept of identity that is both individual and universal, shaped in interaction with others. But his comment also reflects back on us. If Falstaff consists of a variety of personae, this might be equally true for us and our conflicted, multifaceted selfhood.

For the humour scholar Ted Cohen, joking, like a shared game, is first and foremost a social affair.[42] We establish communities based on the joint experience of laughter, bound in mutual pleasure. Cohen believes there is no theoretical foundation for judging whether a joke is offensive or not. Rather than content, context is key. Admittedly, as with all cultural products, we need to strike a balance between the right to free expression and the right to be protected from artefacts that perpetuate hate, as many jokes do. And as in all games, a society agrees on rules to delimit the boundaries of play. But as Falstaff demonstrates, we consist of such a myriad of aspects that in practice it is possible to find a joke funny even if we disapprove of its assumptions—and to accept those who laugh at jokes we ourselves consider unacceptable without necessarily drawing conclusions about their attitudes. Jokes might also remind us to define ourselves through what we share, not what divides us, through communality, not particularistic group attachments. As Cohen hopes, jokes might foster the feeling 'that we are, at least a little, alike'.[43]

This is a hope that Chappelle shares. In 2019, the comedian received the highest comedy award, the Mark Twain Prize for American Humor. During the award ceremony, held at the John F. Kennedy Center for the Performing Arts in Washington, DC, Chappelle talked about his genre, stand-up comedy. He described the community of comedians, which includes comics with widely differing viewpoints, representing the entire spectrum of opinions in the country. Some of them, he realised, were racists. Nonetheless, he recounts, joking momentarily defused the tensions amongst them, and even made it possible to start a debate. In spite of rejecting their views, he tells us, he was able to appreciate their craft.

With their multiperspectival exploration of issues, Shakespeare's plays offer a model for debate in practice. At its best, humour too can make us talk to each other. Shakespeare's comedies do not, as is often claimed, end on the sentimental note of an ideal community. Instead, they are shot through with an ironic awareness of persistent social conflict. The harmony they evoke is always fragile. Nonetheless, Shakespeare deploys humour to forge communities that span particular group affiliations—at least for the duration of the play. This is true for the fictive world as well as for the audience of playgoers in the theatre. Shakespeare's drama demonstrates the range of purposes to which jokes can be put. In the plays, jokes are used as a deadly weapon to devastate others. Alternatively, they are bandied about in verbal jousts by characters attempting to demonstrate their mastery of wit. Jokes can be used to reinforce social norms. Alternatively, by welding laughers into a community, however transitory, humour can foster social cohesion. As Hannah Gadsby points out, joking can help us evade taking a stance. At the same time, humour offers a technique for survival in a world in which the joke is usually on us. In laughing at human nature, we ruefully accept how absurd we are. What jesting also does, both in Shakespeare's plays and in the contemporary world, is to celebrate the power of the human imagination and the pleasures of ordinary life. To make jokes in a manner that affords pleasure to others requires considerable skill, insight, and effort. As Viola says of Feste, 'This is a practice/As full of labour as a wise man's art' (3.1.58–9). Dave Chappelle puts it more succinctly: 'Talking shit is an art.'[44]

NOTES

1 www.theguardian.com/culture/2019/jan/19/is-standup-comedy-doomed-future-of-funny-kevin-hart-louis-ck-nanette

2 William Prynne, *Histrio-mastix. The players scourge, or actors tragaedie* (1633), **8v-***1r. All further references in parentheses.

3 A classic study of anti-stage polemic is Jonas Barish, *The Antitheatrical Prejudice* (Berkeley: University of California Press, 1981).

4 The term 'Puritan' encompassed a range of differing attitudes, but in general it referred to those who advocated a more rigorous reform of the Church of England and were keen to promote a reformation of manners. See Patrick Collinson, *The Elizabethan Puritan Movement* (Berkeley: University of California Press, 1967).

5 Stephen Gosson, *Playes Confuted in five Actions* (1582), C6r.

6 See Peter Lake with Michael Questier, *The Antichrist's Lewd Hat: Protestants, Papists and Players in Post-Reformation England* (New Haven, CT: Yale University Press, 2002).

7 A helpful overview of the range of attitudes towards the ethics of humour is provided in Berys Nigel Gaut, 'Just Joking: The Ethics and Aesthetics of Humor', *Philosophy and Literature* 22.1 (1998): 51–68. Also see the collection of essays in *Ethics and Values in the Information Age*, ed. Joel Rudinow and Anthony Graybosch (Belmont, CA: Wadworth Thomson Learning, 2002), and Carroll, *Humour: A Very Short Introduction*, 76–117.

8 See, for instance, Merrie Bergmann, 'How Many Feminists Does It Take to Make a Joke?' in Rudinow and Graybosch, 187–98.

9 Plato, *Philebus* 48–50, *Laws* 934–36, *Republic* 388–89, 606, in *Plato: Complete Works*, ed. John M. Cooper and D. S. Hutchinson (Indianapolis, IN: Hackett Publishing, 1997).

10 See Thomas Hobbes, *The Elements of Law* (1650), cited in *The Philosophy of Laughter and Humor*, ed. John Morreall (Albany, NY: State University of New York Press, 1987), 20. Morreall's volume provides a useful compilation of the main theories of humour.

11 See Henri Bergson, 'Laughter: An Essay on the Meaning of the Comic', in Morreall, *The Philosophy of Laughter and Humor*, 118.

12 See Freud, *Jokes and Their Relation to the Unconscious*.

13 See excerpts from Immanuel Kant, *Critique of Judgement* (1790), Arthur Schopenhauer, *The World as Will and Idea* (1819), and Søren Kierkegaard,

Concluding Unscientific Postcript to Philosophical Fragments (1846) in Morreall, The Philosophy of Laughter and Humor, 45–50, 51–64, and 83–89.

14 See John Morreall, 'A New Theory of Humor', in Morreall, The Philosophy of Laughter and Humor, 128–38.

15 See Ben Jonson, Discoveries, ed. Lorna Hutson, The Cambridge Edition of the Works of Ben Jonson, Vol. 7, Gen. ed. David Bevington, Martin Butler, and Ian Donaldson (Cambridge: Cambridge University Press, 2012), 590.

16 See A. D. Nuttall, Why Does Tragedy Give Pleasure? (Oxford: Clarendon Press, 1996), 81-105.

17 See Jan Kott, Shakespeare, Our Contemporary, trans. Boleslaw Taborski and Peter Lachmann (1961; New York: Doubleday, 1964).

18 Samuel Beckett, Endgame, A Play in One Act (1957) and Act Without Words 1: A Mime for One Player (New York: Gove/Atlantic, 2009), 26.

19 Friedrich Nietzsche, The Will to Power, trans. Anthony M. Ludovici (Edinburgh: T. N. Foulis, 1909), 74.

20 Hannah Gadsby: Nanette (Netflix Special, 2018).

21 In his Laughter: A Scientific Investigation, neuroscientist Robert Provine takes apart the myth that laughter has medicinal properties. Its main contribution to health is analgesic.

22 See Huston Diehl, 'Disciplining Puritans and Players: Early Modern English Comedy and the Culture of Reform', Religion & Literature 32.2 (2000): 81–104.

23 Patrick Collinson, 'The Theatre Constructs Puritanism', in The Theatrical City: Culture, Theatre and Politics in London, 1576–1649, ed. David L. Smith, Richard Strier, and David Bevington (Cambridge: Cambridge University Press, 1995), 157–69.

24 See Richard L. Greaves, Society and Religion in Elizabethan England (Minneapolis: University of Minnesota Press, 1980), 520–25.

25 Wilson, Art of Rhetoric 165.

26 Sir Thomas More, Utopia, in The Norton Anthology of English Literature, ed. Stephen Greenblatt et al., Vol. 1, 8th ed. (New York: Norton, 2006), 571.

27 Plutarch, Moralia Vol. 8: Table-Talk, trans. Paul A. Clement and Herbert B. Hoffleit, Loeb Classical Library (Cambridge, MA: Harvard University Press, 1969), 629F.

28 Aristotle, The Nicomachean Ethics, 1103b. Also see 2.1-4.

29 See the landmark essay by Anne Barton, 'As You Like It and Twelfth Night: Shakespeare's Sense of an Ending', in Essays, Mainly Shakespearean (Cambridge: Cambridge University Press, 1994), 91–112.

30 *Ricky Gervais: Humanity* (Nexflix Special, 2018).

31 See Margot Heinemann, *Puritanism and Theatre: Thomas Middleton and Opposition Drama under the Early Stuarts* (Cambridge: Cambridge University Press, 1981).

32 Seneca, 'De Constantia Sapientis/On the Firmness of the Wise Man (On Firmness)', in *Moral Essays*, Vol. 1, trans. John W. Basore, Loeb Classical Library (Cambridge, MA: Harvard University Press, 1928), 97.

33 www.nytimes.com/2020/10/26/business/kazakhstan-embraces-borat.html

34 *Dave Chappelle: Sticks & Stones* (Netflix Special, 2019).

35 Johan Huizinga, *Homo Ludens: A Study of the Play Element in Culture* (Boston, MA: Beacon Press, 1959), 13.

36 Michael Mulkay, *On Humour: Its Nature and Place in Modern Society* (Cambridge: Polity, 1988), 37.

37 On humour as a form of play, see Brian Boyd, 'Laughter and Literature: A Play Theory of Humor', *Philosophy and Literature* 28.1 (2004): 1–22. On humour as an imaginary realm, see Gregory Bateson, 'A Theory of Play and Fantasy', in *Steps to an Ecology of Mind: Collected Essays in Anthropology, Psychiatry, Evolution, and Epistemology* (London: Intertext, 1972), 177–93.

38 Ludwig Wittgenstein, *Culture and Value: A Selection from the Posthumous Remains*, ed. G. H. von Wright, trans. Peter Winch (Oxford: Blackwell, 1998), 95e.

39 See 'jest, n.', *Oxford English Dictionary Online*.

40 On metajokes see Carroll, *Humour: A Very Short Introduction*, 24–25.

41 Hugh Grady sees him as the most metatheatrical character in Shakespeare. See Grady, *Shakespeare, Machiavelli, and Montaigne: Power and Subjectivity from Richard II to Hamlet* (New York: Oxford University Press, 2002), 143.

42 Ted Cohen, *Jokes: Philosophical Thoughts on Joking Matters* (Chicago: University of Chicago Press, 1999), 29.

43 Ibid., 29.

44 *The Kennedy Center Mark Twain Prize for American Humor* (Netflix Special, 2020).

Further reading

There is a wealth of literature on humour and the comic. Perhaps a good place to start is with Noel Carroll's *Humour: A Very Short Introduction* (Oxford: Oxford University Press, 2014). Carroll is a leading philosopher of art who has also written illuminating essays on jokes, and on horror and humour. They are included in his book, *Beyond Aesthetics: Philosophical Essays* (Cambridge: Cambridge University Press, 2001). Another excellent introduction to the topic is Terry Eagleton's recent book, *Humour* (New Haven, CT: Yale University Press, 2019), marked by his trademark wit. A further philosophical foray into humour is provided by Simon Critchley's *On Humour* (London: Routledge, 2002). A well-known theorist of humour is John Morreall. He sets out his ideas in *Taking Laughter Seriously* (Albany, NY: State University of New York Press, 1983) and has published numerous works on humour since, including *Comic Relief: A Comprehensive Philosophy of Humor* (Malden, MA: Wiley-Blackwell, 2009). Morreall has also compiled a very useful anthology of humour theory through the ages, titled *A Philosophy of Laughter and Humor* (Albany, NY: State University of New York Press, 1983). A noteworthy essay that sets out the play theory of humour is Brian Boyd's 'Laughter and Literature: A Play Theory of Humor', *Philosophy and Literature* 28 (2004): 1–123. On jokes, Jim Holt's, *Stop Me If You've Heard This:*

A History and Philosophy of Jokes (New York: W. W. Norton, 2008) is an enjoyable and enlightening read. To my mind, the best book on jokes is Ted Cohen's *Jokes: Philosophical Thoughts on Joking Matters* (Chicago: University of Chicago Press, 1999).

Humour has also been investigated from a variety of viewpoints other than philosophy. General studies of the comic include Andrew Stott's *Comedy*, in The New Critical Idiom series (New York: Routledge, 2005) and Matthew Bevis' *Comedy: A Very Short Introduction* (Oxford: Oxford University Press, 2013). Both are wide-ranging and brimful of insights. Of perennial interest is Maurice Charney's *Comedy High and Low: An Introduction to the Experience of Comedy* (1978; New York: Peter Lang, 1987). Two valuable studies on farce are Jessica Milner Davis's book on *Farce* in The Critical Idiom series (London: Methuen 1978) and Albert Bermel's *Farce: A History from Aristophanes to Woody Allen* (New York: Simon & Schuster, 1982). A number of studies take a sociological approach to humour. An outstanding example is Michael Mulkay's *On Humour: Its Nature and Place in Modern Society* (Cambridge: Polity, 1988). Christie Davies' study, *Ethnic Humour Around the World* (Bloomington: Indiana University Press, 1990) is an eye-opener in many ways. He uncovers patterns in ethnic humour throughout the world, such as the urge to project traits like stupidity onto liminal groups. Giselinde Kuipers' *Good Humor, Bad Taste: A Sociology of the Joke* (Berlin: De Gruyter, 2015) draws on the ideas of Pierre Bourdieu in combination with fieldwork research to point to the importance of class in questions of humour. It is also instructive to take account of works such as Mahadev Apte's, *Humour and Laughter: An Anthropological Approach* (Ithaca, NY: Cornell University Press, 1985) and the research findings described in Robert Provine's *Laughter: A Scientific Investigation* (Harmondsworth: Penguin, 2000).

A plethora of ideas on humour from the Renaissance to today is presented in the anthology of excerpts entitled *Reader in Comedy: An Anthology of Theory and Criticism*, ed. Magda Romanska and Alan Ackerman (London: Bloomsbury, 2019). David Galbraith offers a succinct overview of both ancient and early modern theories in his essay, 'Theories of comedy', in *The Cambridge Companion to Shakespearean Comedy*, ed. Alexander Leggatt (Cambridge: Cambridge University Press, 2002), 3–17. An important scholarly work on the Renaissance culture of humour is Chris Holcomb's *Mirth Making: The Rhetorical Discourse on Jesting in Early Modern England* (Columbia, SC: University of South Carolina, 2001), while Pamela Allen Brown's study of a female culture of jesting, *Better a Shrew than a Sheep: Women, Drama and the Culture of Jest in Early Modern England* (Ithaca, NY: Cornell University Press, 2003) is one of the most original studies in the field. A broad view of humour over the centuries emerges from the essays in *A Cultural History of Humour*, edited by Jan Bremmer and Herman Roodenburg (Cambridge: Polity, 1997), while Mary Beard's *Laughter in Ancient Rome: On Joking, Tickling, and Cracking Up* (Berkeley: University of California Press, 2014) offers an inimitable blend of pleasure and erudition.

As regards wit, two scholars whose work in the field is worthy of note are Adam Zucker and Ian Munro. Zucker's *The Places of Wit in Early Modern English Comedy* (Cambridge: Cambridge University Press, 2011) draws on Bourdieu to show how wit is always embedded in material historical contexts. Ian Munro has produced a number of remarkable essays on Renaissance wit, such as a piece on *The Malcontent*, 'Knightly Complements: *The Malcontent* and the Matter of Wit', *English Literary Renaissance* 40.2 (2010): 215–37 and an essay on *Much Ado About Nothing*, 'Shakespeare's Jestbook: Wit, Print, Performance', *English Literary History* Spring 2004 (2004): 89–113. As for clowns, two recent studies worth singling out are Richard Preiss' *Clowning and Authorship in Early Modern Theatre* (Cambridge: Cambridge University Press, 2014) and Robert Hornback's *The English Clown Tradition from the Middle Ages to Shakespeare* (Cambridge: D. S. Brewer, 2009).

Finally, a book that deftly combines a close look at Shakespeare with perceptive readings of contemporary cultural artefacts is Marjorie Garber's *Shakespeare and Modern Culture* (New York: Anchor Books, 2008). In many ways, it offers an early example of the path forged by the series in which this book appears.

Index

Note: Page numbers in *italics* indicate a figure on the corresponding page. Page numbers followed by "n" indicate a note.

alliteration 2, 24
ambivalence 72, 166
Anatomy of Melancholy, The 8
antics, bumbling 2, 3, 139, 148
Antony, Mark (Antonius, Marcus), 56–8, 112–3
Apophthegms 9
Aquinas, Thomas 8
Aristotle 5, 7–8, 51, 159
Armin, Robert 82, 84, 94–5
Art of English Poesy, The 7
Art of Rhetoric, The 7
As You Like It 34, 44, 49, 54, 72, 94
Ascham, Roger 29
Asteismus (Merry Scoff) 7
audacity 30, 105, 122
audience: addressing 33, 112, 118–19, 231; appreciation 14, 30–1; late-night 108; laughter 64, 145, 157; manipulation 31, 33, 64, 82, 87, 123, 125; pleasure/delight, invoking 41, 60, 116, 122; response 5, 25, 59
Augustine of Hippo (St. Augustine) 6

Baron Cohen, Sacha 90–1, 162–3
Beckett, Samuel 151
Book of the Courtier, The 27
Borat Subsequent Moviefilm 91, 162

Borgia, Cesare 122
Bracciolini, Poggio 10, 25
buffoon 8, 25, 85, 88, 94, 138, 146, 159
Burton, Robert 8

Caesar Strabo, Gaius Julius 6
Caesar, Gaius Julius 56
Campbell, Mrs. Patrick (Tanner, Beatrice Rose Stella) 49
Castiglione, Baldassare 27–8, 29, 30, 47n15
Chanel, Macy 92–3
Chapman, George 47n20, 114, 140n4
Chappelle, Dave 163, 164, 164–5, 169–70
Charientismus (Privy Nip) 7
Chettle, Henry 9
Christian, values 6, 55, 97, 144
Cicero, Marcus Tullius 5–6, 24–8, 30, 61, 159
Cleopatra 52, 54, 56–8, 73, 148
clowns: professional entertainers 3, 82–3, 115; sinister 115, 117; social status, low 84, 98; Vice, the 116, 119–20
Coen, Joel and Ethan (Coen brothers) 43, 131, 138

Cohen, Ted 169, 175
Colbert, Stephen 102, 108
Coleridge, Samuel Taylor 128, 130
comedy: art of 18, 95, 152, 154;
   city, genre of 31; contemporary
   161–5, 169; cruel 116–17, 130,
   138, 150; dark/black 131–2,
   138, 149–50; early modern
   6–7, 9, 13, 21–2, 31, 40; female
   3, 53, 67–9; late-night 3, 101,
   108; patterns comedic 15, 50,
   63, 84, 87, 116, 175; romantic
   43; stand-up 3, 13, 67–8, 151,
   165, 169; understanding 4, 13
contemporary: comedians 54,
   68–70, 77, 91–2, 161–3;
   culture 130, 138; society, 23,
   70, 96, 101
Cornwallis, Sir William 12–13
courtesy, rules of 13, 26, 27, 29, 55
crude gags/jokes 91, 130
cultural capital 12, 50, 85
culture: cancel 162, 165; modern,
   early 58, 177; pop (popular)
   3–4, 156

Daily Show, The 102, 102
Dark Knight, The 4, 117, 118, 141n13
De oratore 24, 27, 28, 159
De Quincey, Thomas 128, 130
Death of Stalin, The 106, 106, 107
Dekker, Thomas 9, 14, 31
discourse, as humorous 8, 59, 71,
   166
drama: crime, 131; religious 4, 156
Dryden, John 128, 142n23

Earl of Shaftesbury, third (Cooper,
   Anthony Ashley) 53, 88
early modern era: drama 20,
   116, 118–19; gender/sexual
   references 51–2, 54–6, 58–9,
   63; jestbooks 9–10, 13–14, 30,
   40–1, 58, 60–1, 66, 77, 82;

jesting 3–4, 7–9, 22–3, 32, 58,
   61; wit 3, 5, 8, 13, 20–4, 29,
   33, 38–41
Eliot, Thomas Stearns (T.S.) 81,
   116
Elizabethan: comedians 82, 135;
   female abilities 41
Elton, Ben 95
Endgame 151
entertainment industry 3, 13, 20,
   82, 145
Erasmus, Desiderius 7, 9–10, 27,
   95–8, 148
Essayes 12
ethics: contemporary 143, 145–6;
   puritan 7, 144
euphuism 23–24, 46n8

farce 116, 175
Fargo 4, 131–133, 142n26
female: comedy/comedian
   53–4, 67, 73, 77; early modern
   portrayal of 41, 72–4, 95; fears,
   of male counterparts 41, 67;
   humour, style of 49–50, 68–9,
   176; shame, theme of 69–70
five wits, the 22
Fletcher, Anthony 51–2
flout (Antiphrasis) Broad Flout 7, 144
flyting, ritualized abuse 20, 42
folly: implying 37, 97;
   personification of 95–6, 98,
   148–9; shades of 100, 103–4
fools: professional comedians,
   similarities of 82, 94; self-
   deprecating, depiction of 87,
   96–7, 113, 148
Four Lions 4, 132, 133, 139, 142n27
free expression 145, 169
frump (Micterismus) Fleering
   Frump 7

Gadsby, Hannah 53, 77, 151, 152,
   152–4, 170

Gervais, Ricky 95, 161
Giuliani, Rudolph 91
Globe Theatre 14, 93, 94
Gosson, Stephen 144–5
Gran Torino 18, 19, 20
gullibility 64, 88
gulling 40, 101, 157–8
Gulliver's Travels 88
Gurr, Andrew 82

Hamlet: First Quarto of 15; macabre
    jest 134–7; satire of 132–3;
    surrogate fools of 81–2; urbane
    wit 25
Henry IV Part 1 20, 21, 23
Henry IV Part 2 20, 64
Henry V 20, 114
Henry VI Part 3 73
Henry VIII 30, 55
Heywood, John 9
Heywood, Thomas 31
Hobbes, Thomas 146
Hoby, Sir Thomas 27
House of Cards 4, 122, 124, 124, 138,
    141n18–20
Humanists 10–11, 26, 61
humour: anecdotes 9, 11, 13,
    24, 61, 68; bawdy, as sexual
    innuendo 21, 36, 37, 99–100;
    black 112–13, 121, 135, 137–9,
    140n2; contemporary 4, 15,
    143, 166; crude 91, 126, 130;
    dark, 4, 115, 120–1, 130,
    137, 138–9, 149; derision, as
    5, 50, 138; early modern 7,
    9–12, 20–1, 40–1, 61, 167;
    effects of, past and present 4, 9;
    entertainment industry and 1, 3,
    13, 20, 82, 145; ethics and 143;
    homosexuality as theme 151–4;
    myth of 8, 77, 103, 108, 116;
    pain and 139, 145–6, 149–51,
    153–4; playful 4, 37, 53;
    political 53, 102–3, 106–8, 114,
122, 138, 143; ridicule as 6–7,
    52; social status, as a 29, 33,
    38–9, 43, 148; theorists 28, 67,
    166, 174; ugliness as 5–6, 159
Hundred Merry Tales, A 9, 10, 14, 60
Hutcheson, Francis 52–3, 88

illusion 2, 89, 97, 103, 108, 123,
    130, 167
insults: dim-witted, jests against
    15, 100; friendly banter, as
    18–19, 34, 38; sexual 63; witty
    21, 42–3
Intolerable Cruelty 43, 44
irony/ironic, Ironia (Dry Mock)
    7, 35, 57, 73, 96–9, 121, 126,
    148, 170
Islamic comedy 132–3, 137

Jackson, Michael 163, 165
James I (Stuart, Charles James) 30,
    114
jest/jesting 3; condemned by
    the Church 6, 8; cuckoldry
    references 58–9, 62; jestbook,
    first Renaissance 10–11; playful
    make-believe 4; prowess in 20,
    45, 50; recreation, as source of
    7–8, 9; relationships 33–4, 38,
    41–2; ribald, locker room talk
    21, 38, 85; verbal artistry 9, 22,
    42–3; weapon of attack, as a
    8–9, 14; *see also* jestbooks
jestbooks, early modern era 9–10,
    13–14, 30, 40–1, 58, 60–1, 66,
    77, 82
jester/joker, contemporary
    similarities 4, 115–18,
    149; jokes, repetition of 15;
    professional entertainer 40, 98,
    104, 107, 129, 148
Jests to Make You Merie 14
Jew of Malta, The 116
Joker, the 4, 117–8, 126, 138

jokes: butts of 10–11, 64–5, 88, 119, 130, 145–6, 152; collectors of 9, 159; crackers of 12–13, 147, 157; cuckoldry (betrayal, female) 40, 59, 60, 62, 67, 70–72, 75, 148–9; flirtatious, as 39, 44, 54, 75, 148, 152; linguistic game, as 61, 94; punchlines, delivery of 14, 39, 167; subject matter of, acceptable 2, 5–6, 9, 11, 144, 165

joking relationships: camaraderie, as 18–19, 37–9; flyting, as ritualized abuse 20; power struggle, as a 21

Jones, Spencer 95

Jonson, Ben 31, 114, 116, 147, 158

Julius Caesar 112, 114, 117

Kemp, William (Kempe) 82–4, 93–5

King Lear, 95, 103, 105, 118, 149, 151

Kisin, Konstantin 143–4

Kuipers, Giselinde 49–50, 175

laughable 5, 89

laughter: as best medicine 8; comic response 4, 24–6, 83, 117; creates the humour 28, 147, 157, 159, 169; evokes sexual images 55, 59; relationship driven 51; self-deprecation induced 153–4; uneasy 145–6, 149, 151; women and 50, 62

Lion King, The 134, 139

literalism 2, 165, 167

Lord Chamberlain's Men 82–3, 93, 120

lore: ancient Roman 12; classical 57

Love's Labour's Lost 18, 35, 73, 85, 87, 148, 160

Lucian 96, 110n22

Lyly, John 23, 46n8

Macbeth 127, 128

Macrobius (Macrobius, Ambrosius Theodosius,) 12

Malcontent, The 14, 117, 176

Marlowe, Christopher 44, 116

Marston, John 31, 117

melancholy 8, 41, 160

Merchant of Venice, The 73, 148, 160

Merry Wives of Windsor, The 31, 54, 62, 72, 148

metadramatic 4, 167–8

metajokes 167

metaphorical 35, 37, 134

Middleton, Thomas 31

Midsummer Night's Dream, A 2, 35, 149

mirth 8–9, 55, 58, 63, 65, 128

Mittal, Aditi 68–9, 69

mockery 7, 20, 163

mocking: innuendo 21, 36, 81; of women 59, 68, 75

Moralia 9

More, Sir Thomas 7, 10, 95, 159

Morris, Chris 132, 137–8

Much Ado About Nothing 38–9, 41, 45, 54, 64, 70, 148–9, 160, 176

Mulkay, Michael 166, 175

Munday, Anthony 9, 144

Nanette 151, 152, 153

Nicomachean Ethics, 7

Noah, Trevor 102–3, 108

Othello 66, 118, 149

paradox 8, 9, 94, 97, 101, 149, 154

parody 2, 14, 24, 87–8, 101, 114, 168

Pence, Michael Richard (Mike) 91

Plato, thoughts on humour 90, 146

playwrights 14, 24, 114, 144, 161

Plutarch (Plutarchus, L. Mestrius) 9, 57–8, 114, 159

Poetics 5, 16n6
Praise of Folly 95
prose 75, 130
Provine, Robert 50–1, 175
Prynne, William 144, 161, 165
punchline 14, 39, 167
puns 1, 36, 84, 119, 125, 127, 136
Puritan: critics 144; joke, as basis of 154–5, 156
Puttenham, George 7, 16n10

quick-witted, as desired social skill 12–13, 14, 26, 29, 84
Quintilian, Marcus Fabius 25

Radcliffe-Brown, Alfred 19
Rastell, John 9
religious: conduct 63, 92; conflicts/controversy 136; mockery 10, 15, 22, 97, 129; reformers 13, 158
Renaissance: literature/jestbooks 9, 23, 27, 176; verbal wit 24–6
repartee 12, 21, 25, 31, 33, 37, 73, 84, 148
rhetoric: grandiose 56; persuasive 26; power of 113; Puritan 157; rhetorical sparring/manipulation 7, 20, 24; skill of, 7
Richard III 35, 118, 122, 124, 130, 138, 149
ridicule, humour and 6–7, 52, 81, 90
Roister Doister 8
Roman New Comedy 31, 84
Romeo and Juliet 33–5, 37, 148, 149

sarcasm (Sarcasmus) Bitter Taunt 7
satire 88, 93, 96, 106–8, 114, 117, 132, 138, 148–9
Scholemaster, The 29
Schoolmaster, or Teacher of Table Philosophie, The 11, 12

scoffing 10, 24, 35, 39, 95, 158
self-mockery 97, 148, 162
sexes, battle of: biological differences 51–2, 55; women and wit 3, 29, 38, 49, 51, 53, 56, 62
sexual: abuse, joking about 153, 163, 164; innuendo 21, 37; jealousy 64, 66; urges 146–7
sexual debauchery 145
sexuality, homophobia and 144, 152, 154
Shakespeare's: characters, wittiest are women 3; clowns, use of 86, 88, 117, 148; comedy/comedies 4, 39, 41, 82, 87, 170; drama 23, 73, 151, 170; entertainment industry, birth of 13; fools, 81; humour 3, 5, 15; humour, lack of 1; jokes 1–2; plays 3–4, 22, 29, 34, 54, 56, 82, 88, 149, 170
shame/shameful 5, 69–70
Sir Thomas More 9
sitcom 1, 52
Sly, William 14
social: aspirations 12, 26, 30, 96, 156; climbers 12, 85, 156; injustice 137, 145, 154, 170; interactions 13, 23, 38, 50; media 115, 161–2; norms 32, 148, 170; prestige 29, 31, 37; status 26, 28, 87, 98
soliloquy, self-talk 66, 128
sprezzatura, nonchalance 28–9
St Paul (Paul the Apostle) 8, 97
Sticks and Stones 163, 164
Stone, Lawrence 29–30
Susenbrotus, Joannes 7
Swift, Jonathan 88–90, 93

Tarantino, Quentin 131, 138
Tarlton, Richard 82–3
theatre: critics of 145; play-within-a-play 2, 35, 157, 168

theory: of humour 51, 146, 174; incongruity 147; superiority 146–7
Trump, Donald 91, 103, 108
Twelfth Night 34, 81, 94–5, 100, 103, 155, 158, 160
Two Gentlemen of Verona, The 31, 48n21, 84

Udall, Nicholas 8, 9
Upstart Crow 1–2, 15, 52, 95

van Es, Bart 82
virtue: pursuit of 6, 7, 10, 29, 159–60; reputation of 51, 52, 63
Vives, Juan Luis 55

Webster, John 14, 17n27, 31
White, E. B. 15

Wiles, David 82
Wilkins, George 14
Wilson, Thomas 7, 11, 159
Winter's Tale, The 64, 73
wise fools: caustic wit of 3, 76, 81; characters, Shakespearean 95
wit/wittiness: intellect, as possessing 22–4, 25; social virtue, as a 8; urbane, conversation as desirable 25, 29, 57, 121, 132
witticisms 1, 12, 14, 24, 25
Wolf Hall 2
Wolf, Michelle 53, 54
women: humour, as lacking 49; jests, target of 38
wordplay 9, 147

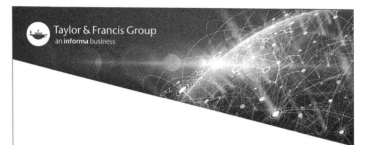

Printed in the United States
by Baker & Taylor Publisher Services